MAKING
THE
MOST
OF
MIDI

Paul Overaa

BOOKMA
PUBLISHI

Making the Most of Midi
by Paul Overaa

Bookmark Publishing Ltd
The Old School
Greenfield
Bedford MK45 5DE
England

Tel 01525 713671
Fax 01525 713716

ISBN 1-85550-006-X

PRINTED IN GREAT BRITAIN

Introduction

I've been working with Midi almost since its inception in the early 80s. Better than that, I've done a lot of my Midi work using PC computers, Atari STs, and the Amiga. That work includes both reviewing and using vast amounts of Midi software, and writing my own Midi utilities. I am using Midi sequencers in a professional capacity, both in the studio and when playing live, so I can throw some light on the practical issues as well as tackling the technical stuff.

Luckily I'm now fully Midi literate and have over a decade of Midi work under my belt. This wasn't always so. I still clearly remember the difficulties I had in the early days, and the questions that I couldn't get answers to. At that time there were few people around who could provide in-depth info. Nowadays things have changed and it is much easier for people to come to terms with Midi and its uses.

There are plenty of Midi books available, so why did I bother to write another? It's because most books which introduce this area do so in ways which are essentially non-technical. The arguments here being that most musicians who want to use Midi are not really interested in what's happening under the surface. My view is that the technical side is too important to dismiss in this way. Why? Because if you know something about how Midi works then many of the things that seem at first almost magical become more understandable. This applies even if you have only a general appreciation of the underlying technical ideas. The techie path, then, has potential benefits for everyone.

I wanted to produce a book which looked at various Midi technical issues but explained them in terms that, with a little perseverance, all Midi users will be able to understand.

In addition I wanted to examine some of the more complex issues, including details about fault finding, how Midi oriented computer programs are written, outlining the internal contents of Midi files, and so on. The aim here being to provide more experienced and technically minded Midi users with footholds into a number of less publicised areas—areas which up until now have been the private domain of Midi experts alone.

How To Use This Book

For the most part chapters are self-contained, but probably best read sequentially.

Chapters 1 to 10 will provide both newcomers and experienced Midi users with a variety of interesting discussions.

Chapters 11 to 15, and the appendices, deal with advanced topics. Because some of this material is of a technical nature I have also provided some simplified explanations which will enable less technically minded readers to make their own footholds in what will at first appear to be complicated subjects. Readers who are new to Midi may prefer to just skim through the bulk of this material initially and concentrate only on the easier preliminary sections.

To get any footholds into these areas at all, however, everyone needs some understanding of what Midi is, what it can do, and why it was developed. So it is with just these topics that we start our journey...

Good luck with your Midi travels!

Paul Overaa, November 1995.

1 Making a Start

We're going to begin by answering the question that all musicians ask initially: What is Midi? From a purely technical viewpoint Midi is a communications scheme that has been designed to allow standardised messages to be passed between pieces of musical equipment (synthesizers, drum machines etc.).

What this means in practice is that Midi allows you to connect together all sorts of different pieces of musical equipment (from any number of manufacturers) and, providing a few ground rules are followed, they'll all work together quite happily. Nowadays it's possible to connect a dozen keyboard synthesizers together in such a way that when you sit at one of them and play something, all the other synths will play the same thing automatically, but perhaps using different sounds.

That in itself is quite an achievement but it is one of the very simplest of the benefits Midi has bought to the world of music. Midi has done far more than this: It has enabled computers to be used to read, store, edit and replay those messages (acting like a digital message tape-recorder) and this has led to a development which has turned the music world upside down...

I'm talking about the Midi sequencer. Not only has sequencing made life easier for the competent musician but it has opened the doors for everyone else. It is no exaggeration to say that the sequencer has made it possible for anyone with the slightest ear for music to play things that sound good without necessarily having to spend years mastering a musical instrument. In many ways the sequencer is to the musician what the word-processor is to the secretary.

Why was Midi developed? This is a bit harder to explain. In fact to explain it at all we need to step back in time and look at some of the things that were happening in the music world just before Midi arrived...

Setting the Scene

You will appreciate the problems that either a lack of standards or a proliferation of non-identical standards can cause. With the early video era we had the format confusion: VHS, Beta, Phillips 2000 and so on. Computer floppy disks going from 8", to 5 1/4" to 3 1/2", coupled with the adoption of many different incompatible formatting schemes, was another nasty many of us could have done without.

Now, if you think the above examples were troublesome you should have seen what was happening in the music business 10-20 years ago. Synthesizers, electronic keyboards with oscillator and sound circuits that could both generate and modify complex sound waveforms, thus mimicking other instruments as well as creating their own special sounds, were beginning to appear. That was great, but incompatibilities between different units spoilt things. Manufacturers would set their own standards for such things as oscillator control voltages and as a direct consequence of this was that linking equipment from different manufacturers was usually a nightmare.

When electronic drum machines came on the scene the situation got worse because many manufacturers chose to adopt different standards for their timing signals.

The real problem was not that any of the manufacturers had chosen bad standards, it was just that because they had chosen different ones, each manufacturer's standards were only coherent within the realms of their own products. From the end-user musician's viewpoint this situation was hopeless because they ended up becoming locked into one particular range of equipment just to get some level of compatibility.

The compatibility issues were seen as a threat to what was expected to become, and in hindsight has become, a major consumer industry. After all... would you nowadays buy a video recorder that had to have a special tape format that was *only* available from the manufacturer of that recorder? Of course you wouldn't!

The early musicians using synthesizers, drum machines and the like were taking the brunt of the compatibility problems. It didn't take too long before the manufacturers realised that something was going to have to be done. Some real effort was going to have to be put into finding a workable, cost effective solution. Within a relatively short time some of the major manufacturers of electronic music equipment, from the States, Germany, Japan, and the U.K. among others, got together to produce a working framework which aimed to allow all types of musical equipment to use a common communications protocol.

The initial ideas and experimental trials seemed to revolve around relatively straightforward instrument-to-instrument links similar to those already in use by companies like Sequential Circuits. Such ideas were quickly replaced, quite possibly by pressure from the high-tech Japanese companies, and a far more adventurous scheme developed which involved the fast serial transfer of data based on the use of optically isolated shielded twisted pair cable links. The cables would be used to transmit information using a well defined, flexible multi-byte message protocol. I'll explain what all that means shortly but the important point to grasp for the moment is just how much musical information was going to be carried by this system. The messages were to cover musical note information, dynamics (measuring how hard keyboard notes were being pressed), internal voice (sound circuitry) selection, pitchbend and modulation effects, and a great many other things besides.

The proposed scheme would also cater directly for the simultaneous control of many different instruments. So as far as musical technology was concerned this was going to be a communications spec second to none. They even gave it a name: the Musical Instrument Digital Interface. Midi!

Some Midi Preliminaries

I'm not going to dive in by giving you loads of technical material. The techie stuff serves little purpose until the underlying ideas have been explained. Having said that, some general info will help because Midi will make sense to you as a musician only if you have a rough idea of how it works and what goes on beneath the surface.

I've already explained that Midi is a musical instrument communications standard. So how exactly do the instruments communicate? Let's deal with the physical connections first.

Midi equipment usually has two or three 5-pin DIN sockets. The terminal marked Midi In is where the equipment receives its Midi information; that marked Midi Out is the terminal from where messages are transmitted. Usually you'll also find something called a Midi Thru socket and this provides a duplicate of whatever is being received at the Midi In terminal. Midi Thru connectors are useful for chaining two or more Midi instruments, a subject that we'll return to in Chapter 3.

For one piece of Midi equipment to communicate with another there needs to be some kind of physical cable connection. The leads used, screened twin-wire cables terminated with 5-pin DIN plugs, are (for obvious reasons) called Midi cables.

You can easily make your own Midi cables, but since they are reasonably priced and readily available from computer and music stores most users buy them ready made.

Making Your Own Midi Cables

Wiring a Midi cable is surprisingly easy if you are handy with a soldering iron. All you need are a couple of 180 degree type 5-pin DIN connectors and a suitable length of thin, screened cable containing two inner wires. Midi cables can be up to 15 metres long, but don't make excessively long cables unless you really need them since they can degrade the shape of the signal pulses passing through them.

The pin in the centre of a DIN plug (pin 2) is used for the earth screen connection, so the screen has to be soldered to the central pin 2 at either end of the lead. The remaining two wires that run through the centre of the cable are then soldered to the pins that are immediately to the left and right of those centre terminals (pins 4 and 5). It is important that each wire is joined to the same numbered pin at each end of the cable—pin 4 to pin 4, pin 5 to pin 5. They should not be cross connected. Both outer DIN connector pins (1 and 3) on both connectors should be left unconnected.

Some 5-pin DIN hi-fi leads, which look very much as though they would double for Midi leads, fail to work as expected. This is often because pins 4 and 5 are cross connected. Other problems can occur with some equipment where leads have inadvertently been acquired which use 4-strand multicore cable with pins 1 and 3 (which should not be connected to anything) being linked.

That takes care of the physical connections, but once connected how do these instruments actually talk to each other? And what exactly is a Midi message? Well, forget about the normal 'Sorry but we're going to be late for the gig because our van has broken down' variety of message. Midi messages have nothing to do with words, phrases or any other kind of text. Midi communications is all done with numbers and the underlying magic here is performed by computer chips.

Midi Communications

The chips used in Midi instruments and all other digital computer equipment involve thousands upon thousands of micro circuits that are basically switches that can exist in one of only two states. It goes without saying that these circuits are very good at representing On/Off, Yes/No,and True/False type situations. Unfortunately they are not much good at anything else and because of this the numbers that computers work with need to be stored and manipulated in a special form that corresponds to these logic circuit on/off type states. The number system associated with this is called binary. It's a system with just two digits—0 and 1.

It should be pretty obvious that in order to represent the normal decimal numbers 0 and 1, only one binary digit or 'bit' needs to be used. But in order to represent larger decimal numbers more bits are needed. Here are a few examples of decimal numbers and their binary equivalents...

Decimal number	Binary number equivalent
0	0
1	1
2	10
3	11
255	1111 1111

So how does all this relate to Midi and those Midi messages? Midi communications are based on the transmission of numbers between 0 and 255, and this entire range of numbers can be stored within an 8-bit binary package which the computer world calls a byte. These bytes can be transmitted through a Midi cable as a series of pulses created by switching circuits that are able to change between their on and off states very quickly—many thousands of times per second.

As far as transmission of 8-bit digital data goes there are actually two different approaches available. You can either use separate wires to carry the individual bits of a given number, so that the whole number is transmitted in one go. Or you can send the individual bits of the number down the same wire one after the other. The first approach is called parallel transmission and though it is potentially faster it suffers from the disadvantage of being more complex electronically, requiring more expensive cables. The second approach, called serial data transmission, is slower but has the important advantage of being cheap and simple.

When the Midi standard was devised everybody involved knew that it would only catch on if Midi equipment, in general, was as affordable as possible. Because of this the manufacturers formulating the standard decided that Midi communications were to be based on serial transmission. Let's get one thing straight. When I was talking about communications speed I was talking relative potential speeds. Midi's serial approach is no slouch. Messages are sent as streams of pulses that travel at a speed of 31.25 kilobaud. That's about one byte of Midi information every 320 millionths of a second!

There are two approaches available for the transmission of pulsed serial data. One approach, which is used extensively for things like computer to printer and computer to modem links, represents the two binary states using different voltages. The RS232C standard for example uses -12v and +12v to represent the two logic states 0 and 1.

The alternative approach, which is the one Midi uses, is based on an electrical current loop and is more akin to sending pulses by switching a light on and off, which is almost exactly what happens. Midi signals do drive a light, or rather a light emitting diode (LED) which is present in every piece of Midi equipment's receiving circuitry. These light pulses are picked up by an adjacent photocell which converts the light pulses back into the pulses representing the digital data.

The LED/ photocell arrangement is therefore able to propagate the switching pulses representing the digital data, whilst providing a physical barrier which prevents current flowing between the various pieces of equipment. This is what is meant by opto-isolation.

Midi's optically isolated closed loop current system has two main benefits. Firstly, it eliminates potential 'earth hum' and other electrical noise problems. Secondly, it is safer than approaches involving direct equipment signal connection.

Midi messages, then, are sent then as streams of bits representing one or more eight bit numbers whose meanings have been defined by the Midi standard. There's nothing magical about this. A group of people simply sat down together and decided what all the various number combinations were to mean. A lot of thought went into the structure of these messages and, once the completed standard was available to follow, the manufacturers of Midi based musical equipment started to manufacture their new instruments with the Midi standard guidelines in mind.

Not all types of Midi equipment are expected to understand all types of Midi messages. Nor does every piece of Midi equipment send every possible type of Midi message, but this doesn't usually cause much in the way of problems - providing you know what types of messages your particular equipment is capable of sending and understanding. More on that later.

I've already mentioned that Midi messages can consist of more than one byte. The first byte, called a status byte, acts as a message identifier and enables the receiving equipment to tell what type of message is coming in. Subsequent bytes of the message, if indeed they exist, are known as data bytes.

Status versus Data

How does Midi distinguish between status bytes and data bytes? It has opted for using the uppermost bit of each byte. Status bytes *always* have the high bit (bit 7) set so these numbers can range from 10000000 binary to 11111111 binary (decimal 128 to decimal 255). Because bit 7 is effectively used as a status byte indicator all data bytes are restricted to values ranging from 00000000 binary to 01111111 binary (decimal 0 to decimal 127).

Midi Channels

Midi recognises the existence of 16 separate channels and a large class of Midi messages, known as Channel messages, contain a channel number encoded within the status byte of the message. Pieces of equipment can therefore be selective about the messages they make use of and the result is that it is possible to have drummers, sequencers, synthesizers etc., all attached to each other via a single Midi communications cable loop. By setting up each unit to respond to a different Midi channel all of the Midi messages can be sent down the same set of cables with each unit responding to only those messages that have the matching channel number identification.

It's a bit like someone writing a letter to you, sticking it in an addressed envelope and posting it - the letter, along with thousands of others, gets carried around the postal system but, as far as reading the contents goes, it is ignored until it arrives at your front door—its final destination. You know the letter is for you because it has got your name and address on it. Midi units know when a channel message has arrived for them because it will have a suitable channel number built into the message's status byte.

Midi at the highest level distinguishes between the channel messages just mentioned and messages of more general interest to the system. You might at this stage be wondering just when all these messages get transmitted. It's usually when you do something - press a note on a synthesizer keyboard, turn a control knob, or select a particular synth voice setting. All of this will be dealt with in the fullness of time but for now we have more pressing things to discuss. Namely, what equipment you need to get started.

2 Basic Equipment

To produce a usable Midi system you need at the very least to have a synthesizer and a sequencer. You can have an awful lot more equipment than this, but these items, along with a couple of Midi leads, provide the starting point that'll get you into the world of Midi. Most of the material in this chapter provides a general overview of the type of facilities available with synthesizers and sequencers, although exact details are obviously going to vary from synthesizer to synthesizer and from sequencer to sequencer. You'll be able to get the specifics from your own manuals—use this chapter just to 'set the scene' as it were.

Synthesizers, in case you've never seen or heard one, are electronic instruments which can create sounds by generating complex sound waveforms. Not only can they be used to invent new sounds but also to mimic other instruments like violins, pianos and drums. They can even duplicate sounds like plates smashing, a person whistling or a helicopter taking off. Synthesizers can change from one sound to another very quickly—one moment your keyboard can be sounding like a violin string section, the next it could be sounding like an oboe, cello or harmonica.

The Midi standard contains one particular class of messages which let this voice changing be carried out automatically, that is without you having to physically change anything on the synthesizer. The snag is, or rather the snag used to be, that these clever synthesizer devices had to be programmed to get the right noises out of them. This, if you were new to such things, turned out to be a difficult and a time-consuming job. Luckily all synthesizers which are on the market nowadays include a collection of pre-programmed voices (presets). These sounds are available from the moment you switch on so you will not need to worry about synthesizer voice programming at all, unless of course you want to!

I ought to mention that nowadays not only can you get Midi keyboard synthesizers but Midi guitars, Midi wind instrument sensors, Midi drum pads and a host of other 'Midi input' devices. Most people, however, whether they are keyboard players or not, tend to start with and continue to use keyboards for the bulk of their Midi work. This being so, most people who are working with Midi tend to a greater or lesser extent to become 'keyboard literate'. Because of this you too are well advised to learn to find your way around a piano style keyboard. Luckily, and perhaps somewhat surprisingly, you definitely do not by any stretch of the imagination need to become a technically competent keyboard player.

There is a very good reason why a keyboard synthesizer is the best 'first instrument' from the beginners viewpoint: Most budget synthesizers, and many more expensive keyboard synthesizers come to that, contain built-in sound circuitry. In effect you are buying the keyboard (which is the Midi input device) and some built-in synthesizer sound circuitry. The sound circuitry serves two purposes. Firstly, it is used to create sounds when you press keys on the keyboard. Secondly, the sound circuits can be 'played' by sending Midi data into the synthesizer via the Midi-In socket.

It is possible nowadays to get keyboards without any sound circuitry, and to get Midi controlled sound modules which are just the synthesizer sound circuitry without the keyboard hardware. The benefit here is flexibility—you can use a single keyboard with many different sound modules, you can change a module without having to change the keyboard... I'll have a look at the benefits of these type of systems later in the book.

Sound expander units like this Roland SC7 Sound Module contain just Midi sensing and sound generating electronics. Because there is no integral keyboard they must be driven by sending them Midi messages from either a separate Midi keyboard or a sequencer.

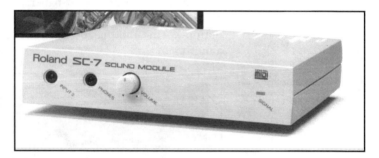

So you are now no doubt asking how much all this gear is going to cost? A synthesizer can cost anything from £50 to £5000. As models get more expensive so the quality of the actual keyboard, the electronic flexibility, and the sounds they make, all get better and better. What does surprise many people is just how good even the cheapest models can sound and the established manufacturers, like Casio and Yamaha for instance, produce some excellent budget ranges!

One thing you will not get with a budget synthesizer will be a touch-sensitive keyboard, that is a keyboard which can sense how hard you press the keys and adjust the volume of the sounds accordingly. Notes will be either on or off (sounding or not sounding) and that, unless you opt for a more expensive touch-sensitive unit, is something you'll have to learn to live with. Unless you are already an experienced keyboard player you are unlikely to worry initially about the difference.

One possibility when looking for a synthesizer is to search for second-hand bargains. Musicians are always changing their equipment and many, once they've got the Midi bug, will often decide to change their original synthesizers for more versatile (and more expensive) models.

This means that there is always a steady stream of adverts in the music magazines and local papers. Often you'll find units at around half the price of the corresponding new model. It's an option worth thinking about if you want to keep initial costs to a minimum.

Casio produce an excellent range of budget synthesizers.

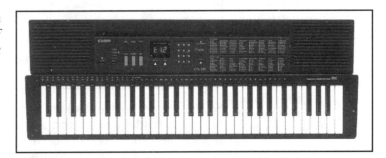

As well as their expensive top-of-the-range professional music products, Yamaha nowadays also provide a variety of less expensive synthesizers.

Synthesizers for serious use do not have any internal speakers so you have to connect them to a separate amplifier/speaker system. Many budget synths nowadays do have a small amplifier and speaker built into them. If this is not the case then for home, low volume use you should be able to avoid further expense by using your hi-fi system.

For Midi work synthesizers need to be polyphonic, able to play many notes at the same time. Eight note polyphony—the ability to play up to eight notes simultaneously—ought to be regarded as the minimum and I'm mentioning this because some very cheap models, even though they are advertised as modern Midi synthesizers, may offer only two or four note polyphonic operation. You'll find these synths limiting right from the start so it would be best to avoid them.

Voices, Sounds and the Midi Connection

The modern day synthesizer can create an enormous variety of sounds. Whether you want the sounds of violins, drums, brass instruments, harmonicas, whistling or dogs barking you can bet your life that even the simplest synthesizer could be programmed to produce good likenesses of such sounds.

With a Midi keyboard digital messages will be transmitted as the keyboard is played. The first point that needs to be made concerns the relationship between the sounds you hear when you play a synthesizer, and the Midi messages which are transmitted. Midi notes themselves are 'timbreless', they are not physically related to any particular sound or synthesizer voice. You can therefore record a melody with your synthesizer set up for a piano sound but if, before playing it back, you change the synthesizer's voice to say a bass-guitar sound then the melody you recorded will play back sounding like a bass-guitar.

The reason I've mentioned this now is that I need to talk about voices, voice selection and the slightly more complicated ideas involved in using the multi-timbral synthesizers that are available nowadays. For a number of reasons this is also a good time to introduce a particularly useful piece of transmittable Midi information called the program change command.

A program change command is a Midi message which allows a synthesizer's current voice to be changed by remote control. A sequencer, by sending such messages, can select suitable synthesizer voices without any manual changes needing to be made to the synthesizer controls. As likely as not your synthesizer will transmit these messages whenever different voices are selected from the instrument's control panel.

Some synthesizers have a fixed program-change/voice relationship so that sending, say, a program-change 1 message will always select one particular voice. Other units employ more flexible arrangements, based on user-definable internally memorised tables. The benefit with this latter approach is that you, the user, can not only choose which voice a particular program change command will select but you may edit and change such tables as and when it becomes useful to do so.

Once a set of voice/program-change-number assignments have been identified or created you'll usually find that the correspondence will work both ways. When, for instance, you manually select voice X on the synthesizer the appropriate Midi program change message will be generated and sent through the Midi Out terminal. Similarly, if that same message is received at the Midi In terminal the synthesizer will automatically change to voice X without you needing to touch any of the synthesizer controls.

The program-change/voice correspondence, then, is essentially numerical, with program change numbers effectively just identifying slots in a synthesizer's voice/program memory. Program change numbers therefore have nothing directly to do with the various audible sounds that a synthesizer can make. The important point is this: As far as the conventional Midi standard is concerned the general relationships between any one particular program change number and the characteristic, audible sound of a particular voice is not defined. On one synthesizer a program change 3 message might select a piano voice, the same message sent to another synthesizer might select an oboe voice.

Program change numbers are often called 'patch numbers'. This stems from the good old days when synthesizers had almost breadboard like connectors with masses of connecting leads being used to route or 'patch in' different parts of the synthesizer circuitry. At a later stage synthesizers became modular and switches were used to route the signals but the 'patch' terminology stuck.

Nowadays even switches are obsolete—synthesizers can store a large number of their settings in memory and these 'programs' can, as we've seen, be selected not only at the touch of a button but by digital messages sent from other Midi devices. Despite the fact that we've moved into this digital synth era, you will still find program change messages being discussed in terms of patch numbers, and the corresponding voice/program combinations being called 'patches'. One minor irritation you might encounter is this: Some synth/sequencer manufacturers tend to use program change numbers 1-128. Others may use 0-127, which is the range of values that Midi uses internally. Because of this you may find that you have to add or subtract one from particular sequencer patch values to get things working properly—for example send a program change 1 command to select the voice which, in your synth manual, is identified as program change 0. It is something that you soon get used to.

Program change messages are extremely useful when creating songs which are to be played using many synths and sound-modules. It is for instance quite common to add program change messages into the start of a sequence so that the right voices/programs are selected just prior to a song being played. They are also frequently used to control other types of Midi units. Digital delay and digital reverb units—gadgets which produce echo, repeat and other sound enhancing effects—are nowadays invariably Midi controlled with different effects usually being selected by sending the unit suitable program change messages.

I almost always start my songs using a four beat count-in sequence which contains the program change messages for selecting keyboard synthesizer voices, drum machine characteristics, programs on the delay units, and voices on any number of sound modules. This ensures that the equipment is automatically set up for the right sounds immediately before the song itself starts playing.

Given the infinitely wide range of sounds that all synthesizers can produce, and the fact that many voice settings are user-programmable anyway, it was not originally thought advisable to implement any scheme which involved associating a given program change number with a particular type of sound. These things were left up to manufacturers to decide upon and this led to all manner of incompatible variations. Basically each user of a particular synth had to find about how the voices of their synthesizer were related to the available range of program change messages.

To a large extent this situation, with a lot of Midi equipment, still remains today. There has however, in recent years, been a significant move towards, amongst other things, the standardisation of a core set of synthesizer sounds. Since these areas are effectively an addition to the existing Midi standard, rather than a fundamental alteration, they have been dealt with separately later in the book. For details see chapter 11 which deals with General Midi and the Roland GS standards.

Previous discussions should nevertheless have given you a good idea of how conventional program change messages can be used. Now comes the rather more difficult job of explaining how these sorts of ideas apply to multi-timbral synthesizers..

The Multi-timbral Equivalent

Synthesizers which can play using more than one voice at the same time are called multi-timbral. The reason these synths are so useful lies in the fact that they can usually be programmed so that different voices respond to different Midi channels, and here there's an important point to be made.

The setting up of a multi-timbral synth is very definitely a function of the synthesizer itself and not directly related to any standard Midi messages as such. As far as the multi-timbral capabilities are concerned it is best to imagine that the synthesizer is not just one synthesizer, but several all rolled into one. Treated as separate logical entities it shouldn't be too hard to imagine that each of these imaginary synthesizers could be set up to receive and transmit Midi data on their own individual Midi channels, and that each could be set to play using a particular voice or group of voices.

How this is done depends on what synth you've got, but rest assured it will always be well explained in the manual. Take the trouble to read about your particular instrument's multi-timbral facilities and spend time experimenting with them—it is important!

Let's suppose for instance that you've set up your synthesizer so that data received on channel 2 is played with a violin/string-section voice, data received on channel 3 is played using a bass-guitar sound, and channel 4 data gets played using a flute sound. What some synthesizers let you do is take any group of such settings and memorise them in a single program location. Having done that they will then allow that multiple setting to be associated with a single program change number.

The end result is that you can not only program the multi-channel/multi-timbral characteristics but you can usually remotely switch between different alternative multi-timbral arrangements by using single program change messages.

Extra Notes on Synthesizer Controls

There are of course a great many other facilities on a typical keyboard synthesizer. You'll find voice selection and editing controls, volume, tuning (for fine control of the overall pitch of the keyboard), transposition options (you may be able to raise or lower the keyboard by an octave or more). There will be levers or wheels for bending the pitches of notes up or down and controlling modulation (automatic cycling pitch variation) effects. Most of the parameter setting, including the Midi oriented options, setting the Midi channel for instance, will be done in conjunction with an LCD display and a few rows of touch switches.

Midi messages can occur whenever you touch either the keyboard or a control, but although all Midi messages are standardised not all synthesizers will understand or transmit every type of message. To find out exactly what message facilities your keyboard has the place to look is your synthesizer manual. In it (probably hidden towards the back) you'll find something called a Midi implementation chart and this will provide a standardised summary of the instrument's facilities (we look at these charts in chapter 7).

One particular control which needs to be mentioned affects the relationship between the synthesizer's internal sound circuitry and the keyboard itself. Nowadays the keyboard-to-sound links are not permanent and in fact many synthesizers provide something called a local on/off control which allows the musician to sever the connection between the keyboard and the sound producing circuitry altogether. From a logical viewpoint this arrangement allows the synthesizer to behave like a separate keyboard and sound module.

When you play a note with the local control off you won't hear anything. That may not appear to be particularly useful but it is. Despite the fact that no sounds will be heard, the Midi information corresponding to the keys and controls being used will still be transmitted via the synthesizer's Midi Out terminal. This, as you'll soon see, helps makes the whole process of selecting and recording various Midi channels, and having them sound with the right voices on your particular Midi set up, a piece of cake and is especially handy when working with a multi-timbral synth.

Here's the basic idea: Most sequencers allow you to both rechannelize and retransmit the data coming into the sequencer. The name that various sequencers give this facility tends to vary. It may be called Midi Thru, Soft Thru, Rechannel, Echo or something else, but I'll stick to calling it an echo-thru facility. On computer based sequencers this echo-thru facility may be available either as a gadget selectable option or menu item that has to be selected. Either way it shouldn't be too difficult to recognise this control from the descriptions provided in the sequencer manual.

The name may vary but the purpose and use doesn't. Echo-thru facilities enable you to send back the Midi data generated by your keyboard, possibly on an alternative channel.

More than that, as you switch channels on the sequencer the incoming Midi data—the data from your keyboard—will usually be rechannelized before it is stored so by using multiple sequencer tracks with the appropriate echo-thru settings you can conveniently record data for all required Midi channels without having to fiddle around with the synthesizer channel/voice controls.

In fact for multi-track/multi-timbral oriented recording the best idea is to select a suitable multi-timbral setting, turn the local control off, and then leave the synthesizer parameter setting controls alone. You then use the sequencer controls to convert all incoming (synthesizer generated) Midi information to the appropriate Midi channel data needed to play the chosen voices on your multi-timbral synth.

The Sequencer

Sequencers come in two basic flavours. Firstly, there are the dedicated standalone sequencers such as the 'black box' units made by Yamaha and Roland. Secondly, there are sequencer programs that have to be run using a separate computer system. The advantage of the standalone integrated units is essentially just portability, although robustness is another quality often mentioned. A major disadvantage is that, in terms of general sequencing, these standalone units are always far more limited in what they can do than the computer plus sequencer program approach.

Make no mistake. If you have a choice it is this latter arrangement that is the best long term pathway to follow although, perhaps unfortunately, it does mean that you will need to become computer literate along the way. This may not be such a bad thing. Computers are not going to go away and everyone should know something about them.

Newcomers to computing often tend to look at hardware first and then, having chosen a set up, buy it. Only then do they look for the software they want. This is definitely doing things the wrong way around because to a large extent the ability of a computer to carry out a particular job—whether it be word processing, accounting or Midi sequencing—depends more on the software being run than the hardware running it.

Nevertheless, the hardware is important and although it would be out of place in a book of this nature to talk too much about computer hardware, some notes may be useful.

Choosing Computer Hardware

Firstly, all 8-bit machines (C64, C128, BBC Model B and so on) should be regarded as obsolete and should definitely not be purchased by anyone thinking of getting a computer for sequencing use. Let me hasten to add that this is not because these machines cannot be used for Midi (in fact some of the first Midi software I ever wrote was written for a C64). The fact of the matter is simply that time and computer technology marches on and 8-bit technology is now well and truly dead.

Nowadays we're talking about 16-bit computers, and four categories of machines come readily to mind: The Atari ST and Falcon machines, the mass of PC clones, The Apple Macintosh range, and the Amiga series.

What can I say? The Atari ST machines are cost effective. Because these machines came with Midi ports as standard right from the word go, a massive base of musician users developed. This established user base encouraged a great many software companies to produce sequencer packages for the ST and the result is that a lot of good Midi software is available.

The Falcon, a relatively new machine, is essentially a more modern replacement for the ST. Since the Falcon can run most ST software it probably will do well but this sort of compatibility, though important, may not always ensure success. Atari did develop a portable Mega ST type computer, called the Stacey, and I was probably one of the few musicians who ever got to use a Stacey for Midi on live gig work. The machine performed very well but for a number of reasons it did not become popular and was effectively dropped from the Atari range shortly after its release.

The Stacey should have done well because it ran ST software unchanged—after all, it was essentially an ST machine. With manufacturers in general however there is a lesson to be learnt—the moral is not to jump in and buy the latest Super-Whizzo Mark X to beat all Super Whizzos until you are sure that the new machine develops a reasonably sized user base. This is a matter of practicality—with machines that, for any reasons, fail to be popular there will invariably be fewer hardware add-ons, less support in magazines and so on.

The Atari ST has formed the basis of countless Midi sequencing set ups.

The Falcon, the latest offering from Atari, can run existing ST software.

PCs? These machines just will not lay down and die, despite the fact that in many programmers' opinions their internal architecture should have resulted in obsolescence years ago. There is a saying amongst business users that no one ever got fired for buying a PC. It is as valid to day as it ever was. PCs then are as popular as ever, and with the newer and faster 486 machines now available at quite reasonable prices the interest in PC based Midi sequencing is growing substantially.

The PC is growing in popularity amongst musicans and there is now plenty of good music software around.

Last, but not least comes the Amiga. I love these machines. Technically they are superb. As a musician, however, I'll be the first to admit that the Amiga has had an uphill struggle music-wise, although all the signs are that this is beginning to change. The Amiga was let down initially because of the limited variety of Midi software available (much less than on say the Atari ST). Because there was less software, fewer musicians tended to opt for an Amiga-based solution to their Midi needs. This smaller music-oriented user base meant that a lot of the established, top end, Midi sequencing software houses were afraid to commit themselves to the Amiga marketplace. Catch 22 again!

Two companies, Dr T's and Blue Ribbon Soundworks, have provided and supported good Amiga sequencing software for many years. With the Amiga now becoming a little more credible in the music arena there is at last real evidence that their faith in this machine is beginning to pay off.

The Blue Ribbon Soundworks Bars & Pipes sequencer is ideal for video/multimedia oriented Amiga music applications.

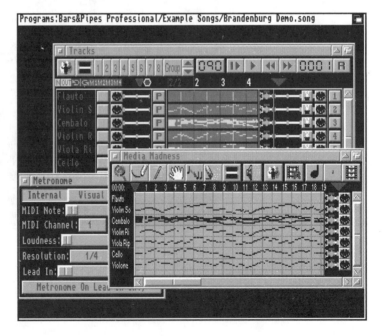

Whatever machine you go for there are, budget permitting, some general points worth making. If at all possible get a system with a hard disk—never go for anything less than 80Mb and if possible opt for 200Mb or more.

As far as computer memory is concerned - also get as much as possible. If, because of budget considerations, you do have to get a machine with only a megabyte or so of memory, then get make sure that you can fit extra memory at a later stage. Heavyweight sequencing packages often require a lot of computer memory and you may find that if you upgrade to a more powerful sequencer, extra ram may be needed in order to use the thing.

There are other considerations that should be mentioned for completeness. A number of companies are now producing add-on cards with multiple, independent serial outputs that allow a number of quite separate Midi-Out ports to be driven at the same time. The aim here being to increase the effective number of available Midi channels from 16 to 32, 48 and so on. This approach is useful in professional studios but you usually need fast, top of the range computer hardware to get the best results. Such boards also tie you to the particular software packages which support them and that is a point worth bearing in mind. Whilst there are a few professional applications which benefit from these multiple port approaches, my opinion is that wholesale moves of the Midi community in these directions at the moment are unnecessary.

When the next generation of even faster computers comes along this situation could, and probably will, change.

Dr T's KCS is one of the best Amiga sequencers for serious use.

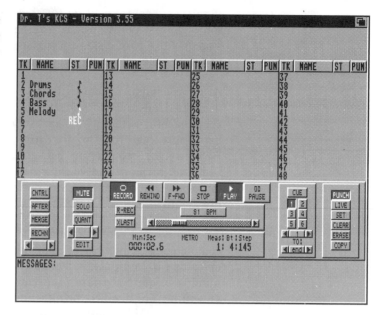

The final choice you make hardware-wise will depend on many things. Available cash, potential other uses of the computer and so on. Most books will kid you otherwise, but the bottom line is that there is no easy answer as to what computer to buy. I could play safe of course and tell you to go out and buy a top of the range, devastatingly powerful, machine. But that would be a bit like recommending a very expensive sledgehammer for everyone regardless of the fact that some people will only want to crack nuts with it.

In reality much will depend on what you, as a Midi user, will expect to be able to do. Check out systems that you think may be suitable—and affordable—and be wary of what the dealers themselves tell you until you confirm things from other sources. Ask friends, read relevant magazine reviews and build up a general understanding of the available options.

In other words, adopt much the same approach as if you were buying a car or anything else. A second-hand Atari ST, perhaps one that was originally bundled with the Steingberg Pro 24 sequencer, can provide a cheap, but still perfectly usable, entry point for the user on a tight budget. In short, you do not necessarily have to spend a fortune.

Choosing The Software

So much for computer hardware buying guidelines. The other step, and remember that this step should come first if you have yet to buy a computer, is to get—or at least choose—some sequencing software. Often, of course, a user may already have a computer for home or business use and simply get to a point where they ask: What Midi sequencing software can I get for my machine?

Sequencer programs can cost anywhere between £40 and £600. Nowadays there are quite a few to choose from. Steinberg's Cubase is one of the established heavyweight sequencers used by professional studios, Pro 24, an older sequencer that was bundled with Atari ST music packages for a long time, also still has a large user base. Lower down the scale Sound Technology's Sequencer One Plus is a good budget priced offering that is available on both the Atari ST and the Amiga. I use Dr T's KCS and Bars & Pipes Professional for most of my Amiga Midi work. I'll talk more about the possible options later but, if you are a Midi newcomer, then for the moment I wouldn't suggest diving in and buying a top end sequencer program. Aim initially for one of the simpler packages because you'll find them easier to use.

There are a number of public domain Midi software packages floating around but to be honest I've never seen anything sequencer-wise that I can truthfully say I'd be happy to recommend.

Irrespective of cost, all sequencers will offer a set of core facilities that will enable you to record Midi data from your synthesizer and play it back. They will also provide a mass of editing options that let you copy sections of music, transpose (change the key), add notes, delete notes... If your timing was a bit wrong you can even ask the sequencer to correct (quantize) the timing of the notes for you.

A great many sequencers adopt a tape-deck style approach to Midi record/playback operations. The analogy is a good one because conceptually a sequencer is very much like a multi-track tape recorder. The main difference being that it records digital Midi messages rather than audio sounds. Most sequencers actually make the analogy very clear and the display will contains buttons for play, record, fast forward, rewind and so on, all serving similar purposes to the equivalent controls found on a conventional tape recorder.

Steinberg's Cubase is a high-powered sequencer used by professional musicians.

As likely as not your sequencer will load up with a set of default settings available which make initial record/play operations straightforward. There is also likely to be an introductory tutorial in the manual which you should read and work through. The chances are that this will be quite sufficient to get you started but in case you do hit problems, here are a few general notes that may help...

One sequencer setting that may need to be checked or altered concerns the clock/timing facilities, which is sometimes labelled as internal/external sync or some similar term.

Most sequencers can use either their internal clock as a musical timekeeper or they can use special incoming Midi messages known as 'Midi clocks' which are transmitted by some Midi devices such as drum machines. Although some keyboards do have Midi clock generators on board, the chances are that your synthesizer will not so you will need to check and, if not already active, select the 'internal clock' or 'internal sync' options on the sequencer.

If there is a choice of metronome settings you should (initially at least) opt for an ordinary audio output, one which produces an audible click to help you keep time. You'll know when you've got these settings right because when you hit Play you will hear the metronome clicking away and will probably see a bar measure indicator increasing with each click. At this time you can experiment with the tempo control. By altering the value (which may involve typing in a new value or using the mouse to drag-select a new value) you'll be able to alter the speed at which the sequencer records and plays. The idea here is that you adjust the speed of the metronome until it is the same speed as the music you wish to play. Four clicks of the metronome for instance will then be equivalent to four beats of your music, one bar of music in 4/4 time, that is.

It may be also possible to set a 'count in'—choose to have a number of metronome clicks sound before the sequencer starts recording that is—or have the sequencer start recording automatically the moment you press a note on the keyboard or touch a synthesizer control.

Similarly, some sequencers offer an auto-loop facility whereby when they get to the end of a certain user-defined number of bars they loop back to the beginning and start playing them again, perhaps recording any new data on another track. To use this loop facility you may need to set a track length value, which might be done using either the sequencer's menu or some separate selectable 'set-up parameters' page.

Modern sequencers have so many functions and so many different ways of implementing those functions that it's hazardous to give definite guidelines as to what to look for. Graphics-style programmable tempo changes using a tempo map and tempo tap options, which enable you to set the tempo by tapping on a note or drum pad, are useful as is having a variety of metronmome options—audible clicks, particular midi notes and the like. Non-destructive editing or 'undo buffers' which enable you to reverse otherwise permanent changes are handy, as are options for being able to offset a complete track by one or more Midi clocks.

Nowadays, however, so many of these things are provided as standard and it is rare to find a sequencer that is unable to do a good job, especially since as you get used to a particular sequencer or software package you'll learn ways to get around any apparent shortcomings.

Most computer based sequencers provide special display pages that let you set up important global settings. One useful extra that the Dr T's KCS sequencer provides is a 'transposition protected' drum channel.

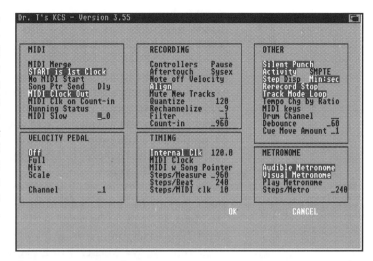

Computers and Live Bands

One of the arguments in favour of standalone, dedicated sequencers is that they are built with the rigors of being on the road in mind. This is undoubtedly so, but it may surprise you to know that for many years I've been taking PCs, Atari STs, and even Amigas out on live gigs (but not all together). Needless to say you have to be a little careful but modern computers are far more robust than many people think. Most of the machines used have been floppy disk based and I have always made a point of taking with me several backups of both my sequencing programs and the data disks holding the sequences. In the early days I was too worried about the fragility, and therefore the reliability, of hard drives to risk dragging hard disk based machines around. Hard disks used to be very temperamental.

The first hard disk computer I used live was the Atari Stacey. This behaved extremely well and after this time I became less pessimistic. Modern hard disks are far more robust than they used to be. This stems mainly from the research that went into producing reliable drives for portable machines.

I would however recommend that all users who take hard disk based machines out on gigs also carry floppy backups of software and sequences—just in case of trouble.

Most of the facilities provided by modern day sequencers are related to sequence editing. This sort of power isn't needed when you just want to play existing sequences that you've created. When you are playing live you really want things to be as simple as possible and one solution that is often adopted is to store all of your sequences in Midi file form and then use a Midi file player for live performances. Rack mounted and stand alone Midi player units are readily available nowadays and at least one company has produced a Midi file player that works using the Atari ST without its monitor. There is a freely distributable Midi file player program—Midi Player—available to Amiga users running Workbench 2 or higher. This appeared because I needed a Midi file player program for the Amiga and couldn't find one in the public domain. To cut a long story short, I ended up writing the software myself!

Paul Overaa's
MidiPlayer
program offers
easy Midi file
playing for Amiga
users.

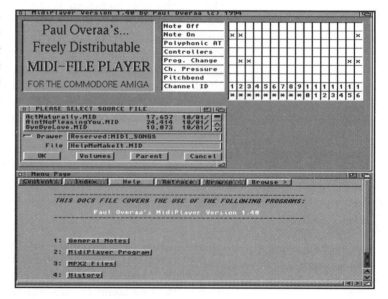

3 Making the Right Connections

In terms of linking a simple two piece sequencer and synthesizer system, there is usually nothing to it. You take one Midi lead from the Midi-Out of the synthesizer to the Midi-In of the computer or standalone sequencer. This will be the lead that carries data from the synthesizer to the sequencer or sequencer program. Connect a second cable from the Midi-Out of the sequencer to the Midi-In terminal of the synthesizer—it is down this lead that the sequencer will send information to the synthesizer. Switch on, then, if you are using a computer-based sequencer, load your sequencer program according to the instructions given in the sequencer manual.

With more complex set ups there are a few other things to consider and that's what we are now going to look at...

When Your Midi System Starts To Grow

One of the great things about Midi is that it allows for virtually unlimited expandability. You may start with a sequencer and a single keyboard synthesizer but at a later stage decide that you'd like better, or a greater number of, synth voices available.

To do this you don't necessarily have to go out and buy a new keyboard synth (unless a better keyboard is needed as well). Instead you can buy a synth expander unit, a box which contains all the Midi driveable sound-producing circuitry but without a keyboard.

There's plenty of other goodies as well. Drum and percussion machines which can be used to both generate Midi data and act as percussion sound sources when being driven by a sequencer. Midi controllable digital effects units. For the pro's there are even things like Midi controlled mixing desks, Midi controlled lighting rigs and so on.

Philip Rees are one of a number of companies that produce a range of Midi Thru/Merge boxes.

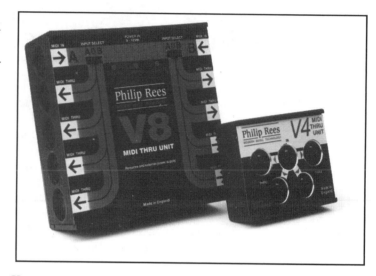

You control expanders in much the same way as conventional Midi keyboard synths but relative to fully fledged keyboards expanders have two advantages. Firstly, they are cheaper than the corresponding equivalent synthesizers. Secondly, they are physically much smaller, with many being designed to fit the standard rack mounting systems used by professional musicians. With many expanders now only requiring 1U of rack space a 12U sized flight case can hold as many as a dozen separate rack mounted synthesisizers.

These rack mounting units are also ideal in another respect because most of the inter-unit Midi cabling can be permanently set up inside the case. If you are a working musician and ever go down this particular equipment path, make sure you get flight cases that are accessible from both front and back because if a lead becomes disconnected—due to vibration whilst in transit say—or some other fault occurs ,it is essential to be able to get to the back area of the expander units easily. That's where all the Midi and power connections will be situated.

Another tip that has absolutely nothing to do with Midi, but is useful all the same, is to carry a torch with you. Once the stage lights are down then even with an open back flight case it can still be a devil of a job hunting around inside without some extra light on the subject. Remember - connectors and plugs, Midi cables, rack and the mounted equipment itself are often all coloured black!

Now, having whetted your appetite with talk of all this equipment it is time to see how Midi units can be physically joined and to mention some of the snags that are sometimes encountered. With three or four pieces of Midi equipment, and no sequencer, linking them is easy. You just 'chain' the devices using the Midi Thru terminals as shown in figure 3.1.

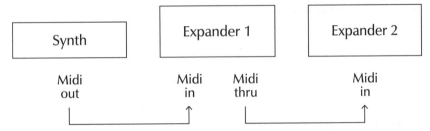

Figure 3.1: Chaining multiple Midi units.

The same sort of thing may be done when playing with sequencer driven set ups and, providing all of your units—or all except the last one in the chain—have Thru connections, three or four units can usually be linked without problem. You cannot, however, link Midi equipment in this so-called 'daisy chain' way ad infinitum because each time the Midi signal passes through a unit a slight deterioratation in signal quality will occur. At some point the Midi signals reaching the units at the end of the equipment chain become distorted enough to be unrecognisable, and then troubles develop. Notes get stuck or missed, rogue messages appear and so on.

The way to avoid difficulties is simple. Instead of chaining Midi units as just described, you adopt an arrangement known as a 'star network' in which each Midi unit gets its own direct path to the Midi data stream source. This approach is used in many sequencer based record/play situations and some standalone sequencers provide a number of Midi Out terminals especially for this purpose. Figure 3.2 shows a typical example. Doing things this way means that the Midi signal travels to each unit along a separate path so excessive signal degradation is avoided.

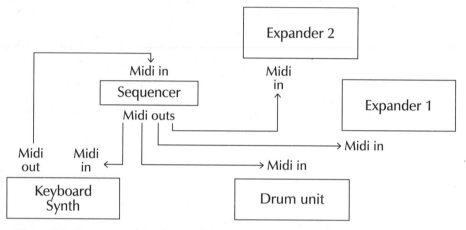

Figure 3.2: Star networking is easy if the sequencer has multiple Midi Out terminals.

The bad news here is that many sequencers and computer Midi interfaces are not provided with multiple Midi Out terminals. And because of the nature of Midi's digital signals it is not possible to solve the problem by splitting up a conventional Midi lead to produce one with multiple connections on one end. The solution here is to use a device known as a Thru box which enables you to turn a single Midi Out connection into any number of outputs. The result is the connection arrangement shown in Figure 3.3.

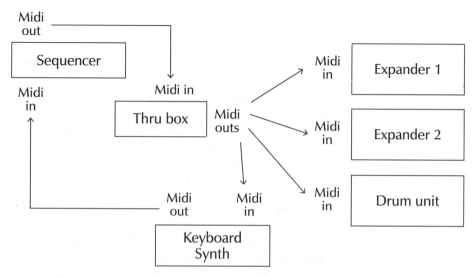

Figure 3.3: A typical star network arrangement using a Midi Thru Box.

Many companies now produce Thru boxes. Some, often battery driven, will offer only two or three Midi Out terminals. Others may provide 10 or more Midi Outs and these usually tend to be mains powered units which have their own built-in transformer and power supplies. There's not a lot you can say about Midi Thru Boxes, other than the fact that they work. I've never found one that didn't do the job it was supposed to. Basically you plug them in and forget about them—it's as simple as that.

It is however worth mentioning that when you get to the stage where you need a Thru box - get one with a few more Midi Outs than you need at the time. This will give you a little more flexibility for expansion.

The golden rule with all of this Midi connection stuff is: Midi Outs and Midi Thrus are terminals which transmit Midi data so if either a Midi Out or a Midi Thru terminal is connected at all, then it must always be connected to a Midi In—to a Midi data 'receiver' terminal, that is. The direct connection of two Midi Ins, two Midi Outs, or Two Midi Thrus cannot possibly ever work and if you think about the purposes of the Midi In, Midi Out and Midi Thru terminals you'll never knowingly make such mistakes. Trust me—you'll still occasionally do it accidentally though!

There is one point about 'chaining' and 'star' arrangements that is fairly obvious but perhaps deserves a mention. You do not have to use one or the other, you can use a combination. If, for instance, you've got a five output Thru box and six units to connect, you can use a basic star network coupled with a short chain as in Figure 3.4.

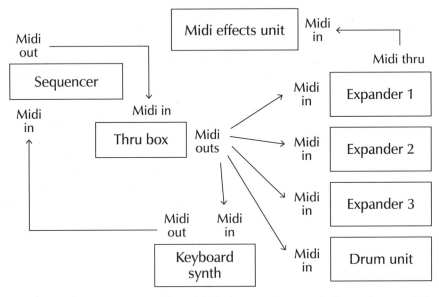

Figure 3.4: Combining star networks with chain arrangements is fine, as long as chains are kept short.

Merge Units

Whilst the conventional Thru box solves a lot of Midi connection problems, it doesn't solve them all. Sometimes you may need to combine Midi signals from two or more sources. You might for example want to use both a keyboard synthesizer and a drum machine as input devices at the same time...

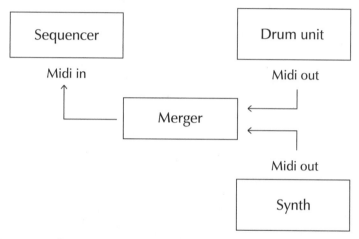

Figure 3.5: Merge units are necessary to combine multiple Midi sources.

Similarly, on a live gig you might need to use an expander with both a keyboard synth and some Midi drum pads. Or perhaps a number of Midi keyboards need to share the same set of expander modules (this is also often needed in studio based set ups). Many companies produce boxes which let you do all of these types of things. They're usually known as dual or triple input merge boxes and basically they allow you to combine two or three completely separate Midi data streams and routine them to various outputs. A schematic 'two in, five out' arrangement is shown in Figure 3.6.

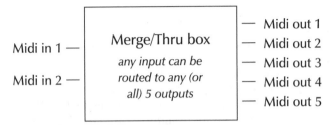

Figure 3.6: This type of Merge/Thru box arrangement would allow you to merge and distribute twin Midi data streams into five Midi Outs.

The merging of multiple streams of Midi messages is a relatively complicated procedure because the ordering of the bytes of information has to be done in such a way that the organisation of each received message from each input stream remains intact. Naturally, these types of units are more expensive than those which offer simpler arrangements. Providing you can afford the extra cash these boxes will give you more flexibility.

Talking Personally

When it comes to linking different Midi units we enter an area which to some extent has a touch of magic about it. I have six rack-mounted Midi units which for live gigs are permanently chained together without any thru boxes at all. The point of interest here is that I experience none of the problems that are normally associated with such long chains of Midi equipment. The leads inside the flight case have been kept as short as possible since this helps to minimise potential signal degradation.

I know from experience however that I am pushing things in this respect, but I'm happy to do so because I know that the arrangement I've adopted works for my equipment and I did all sorts of experiments to convince myself that I had chosen the optimum physical order of Midi units.

The optimum physical *what*? Yes, if you do want to push your Midi luck in this respect you are almost certain to find that even changing the order in which you connect the units could make a difference as far as the presence or absence of Midi signal degradation problems is concerned. I have for instance got an old MidiVerb delay unit which always goes at the end of my equipment chain. I've found that if I place it at the front of the chain (so that the sequencer data passes through the MidiVerb unit first) I start to get errors from a Casio expander unit further down the chain.

In my studio, where many different pieces of equipment are in use from day to day, I simply do not take those kind of liberties and calculated risks. I always use a star network arrangement and always have a collection of Thru/merge boxes and switching units in use.

Midi Switchers

A Midi switcher or switch box enables one of a number of possible inputs to be selected and passed through the unit.

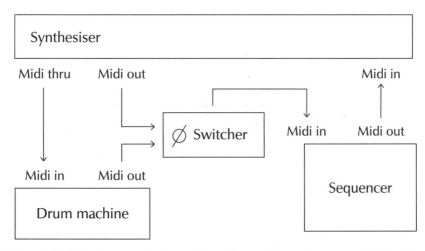

Figure 3.7: Switchers can eliminate the need to unplug and rearrange Midi cables.

They're useful because they eliminate the need to alter your Midi wiring when you want to switch input devices. At times you might for instance want to use either a keyboard synth or a drum machine as the Midi input device. The switcher arangement shown in figure 3.7 allows you to do just that without ever needing to unplug and rearrange Midi leads.

Switchers are cheap, simple devices that are essentially just conventional electrical switches. As such they can also be used the other way round, like this...

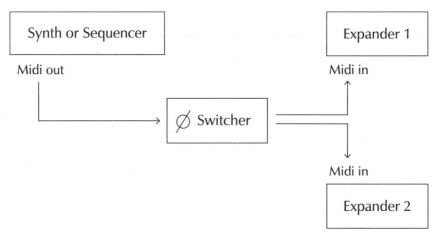

Figure 3.8: Possible alternative use of a Midi switcher.

These arrangements are not particularly useful given that normally all expanders would be set to their own individual Midi channels anyway.

Midi Patchbays

One of the most useful boxes for Midi studio use is a thing called a Midi patchbay. This is a more sophisticated switcher unit which lets you switch select the routing configuration of a number of Midi inputs and outputs. The system that I use is a modular one based on units that control five Midi Ins and five Midi Outs. Its primary use is to eliminate the constant plugging and unplugging of leads when using different Midi units. Patchbays can also function as user configurable Thru boxes although, relative to simple Thru boxes, they are expensive. But when you arrive at the stage where you are collecting a growing array of Midi equipment you'll find that such units come in very handy. You can get Midi controllable, electronic patchbays which allow large numbers of user-programmed signal routing arrangments to be set up and selected. These units are rather expensive and tend only to be used in professional studios.

Last Words

As far as connection schemes are concerned the Midi newcomer needs to be a bit wary about collecting gadgets for the sake of it. My advice is to always aim to keep the cost down as much as possible - after all, there is absolutely no point in buying things if they are not needed. No matter what Midi gear you collect your first task should be to experiment with your own equipment and see exactly what you can and cannot get away with. You'll then be in a position to decide exactly what types of Thru/merge/switching facilities will best suit your Midi set up.

Some musical equipment can have its internal settings changed via Midi. A guitar amplifier for instance might have program change selectable lead/rhythm channels and chorus/reverb effects. Unless a sequencer is already in use in the band or studio set up concerned it is not necessary to incorporate, or have the expense of buying, a sequencer just to provide Midi messages for simple equipment control applications. There are plenty of programmable Midi footpedals and controller boards available nowadays which can be configured to generate program change messages .

Many other connection related devices are available to the Midi user. Line driver units that can provide Midi communications over much longer distances than Midi itself can cope with (1000 metres or more) are useful for PA companies and large studios. Specialist Midi/CV converter units can enable analogue synthesizers or CV samplers to be controlled via Midi.

4 How Your Sequencer Works

So far we've introduced Midi's serial communications, learnt something about the equipment used, and seen the ways in which Midi systems can be connected. The computer plays a big part in all this because all sequencers, whether they are based on the use of separate computers or dedicated standalone units, will at the end of the day use micro-processor chips to store and manipulate the information which your Midi equipment will provide.

This computer-music connection can seem a bit like magic so it's worth spending a bit of time seeing exactly what goes on inside a sequencer program and seeing how things like key changing and quantizing relates to the messages transmitted by a synthesizer.

As you now know, the things which make message transmission possible are the Midi terminals we've talked about. These terminals transmit and receive Midi messages and it is these messages which sequencers use to collect the information about what you are playing. When do these numbers get transmitted? It's usually when you do something—touch a control knob, press a note on a keyboard... If for instance you press the Start button on a Yamaha RX11 drum machine then a 'start' message, actually the number 250, will be transmitted followed by numbers which represent the drum notes.

On a synthesizer, streams of numbers which represent such things as the notes being played and controller information, will be transmitted at the Midi-Out terminal. Other types of Midi equipment send similar streams of numbers and because the meanings of the numbers are standardised one piece of Midi equipment is able to understand the messages from another piece of equipment. To get one unit to 'talk' to another you simply use a Midi lead to connect them using the appropriate Midi In and Midi Out terminals.

When you connect a sequencer into a Midi system it is able to 'read' all of the Midi messages and 'record' what is going on as you play. Sequencers are not interested in the sounds being made, it's the Midi messages, the streams of numbers, that hold the magic key.

When you hit a note on a synthesizer keyboard three pieces of Midi data actually get transmitted... a status byte which says 'here comes a message about a note being hit', a number representing the particular note in question, and lastly a number which indicates how hard the note was hit—non-touch sensitive keyboards transmit the fixed value 64 here. The status byte includes details of which Midi channel is being used so after a sequencer has read these three pieces of data it will know firstly that you've hit a note on the keyboard, secondly it will know which Midi channel you're using, thirdly it will know which note you hit and lastly it will have a measure of its volume.

This type of information gets stored initially in the computer's memory - usually as a simple list of events. A bit more information needs to be added before the sequencer can make use of this data - it needs to know something about the time scale between various events, otherwise it wouldn't be able to play them back in the right way. Sequencers can usually do several things here... firstly they can use their own 'clock' to keep track of the time between events, secondly they can read an external Midi clock, which you the user must provide. A Midi clock is a Midi message whose sole purpose is to create a 'system time' which can be read and interpreted by all connected equipment.

So, one way or the other the sequencer can recognise the time interval between the various Midi events which are occurring and it is therefore able to 'time stamp' each event. This means that the computer knows not only that you have pressed a note on the keyboard, but it has kept a record of when you did it.

This pattern of events occurs for all of the Midi messages which are received and, at the end of the day, the sequencer will have built a list of all the messages and details of the times at which they have occurred. To replay such a sequence all that the sequencer needs to do is read through this list of events and play back each event at the right time. To increase the tempo it will play the events back faster, to decrease the tempo it does the opposite. Because all of the event information is in number form it's easy to modify - to transpose a sequence upwards by one semitone it will just add 1 to each note value, to transpose downwards by an octave it will subtract 12 from each note number. It's as simple as that!

Duplication is just as easy. To copy a section of Midi data the sequencer will read the part of its memory which holds the necessary information and copy it to another area of its memory. To quantize a list of events it will read all of the time stamps and round them up or down to fit in with whatever quantize value you've selected.

Tracks, sequences, complete songs etc., are all handled in the same sort of way and although specific details of the internal formats used do vary, the basic ideas are essentially the same. Sequencers work with numbers - reading, manipulating, storing and transmitting them according to predefined rules. For the sequencer at least, the world of Midi is a silent world of addition, subtraction and event manipulation—not that far removed from the operations of a sophisticated calculator.

Some sequencers allow you to view detailed lists of the Midi events stored in memory.

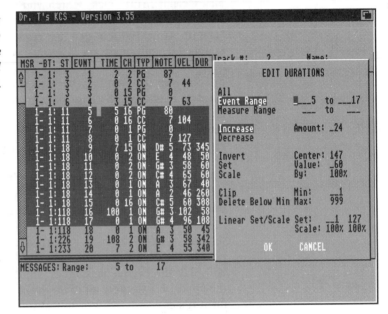

Sequence Editing

All sequencers provide facilities which allow the stored 'events' that represent the various Midi messages to be viewed and edited. The exact way that this is done varies greatly from sequencer to sequencer. Sequencers not only vary enormously in terms of the editing facilities they provide, but also in the names they give to the various editing options. Fortunately, the more common editing functions, those which tend to be available on most sequencers, are usually easy enough to identify from the manual descriptions of what they do.

The term 'editing' usually implies making changes to track or sequence data after it has been recorded. In practice the user also has some control over both the type of data to be recorded and the way that existing track/sequence data should be replayed. The usual arrangement is that the sequencer will have a special 'global parameters' page, or list of menu options, whose settings will govern the way the sequencer actually behaves during use. It's here that the user can decide whether the sequencer should use an internal or an external clock, whether it should provide an audible metronome click or not, whether it should continuously loop through an N-bar sequence or not, and so on.

Other settings may involve things like being able to protect a Midi channel from being transposed, automatically sending Midi start messages, or inserting gaps between groups of messages which might otherwise be sent as unnecessarily dense packets of Midi data.

In addition to all this there may be any number of pre-record and post-record parameters and effects which can be selected. The difference between these two classes of controls is well worth mentioning: Pre-record parameters will govern the type of data actually stored in the tracks and sequences. Post-record parameters govern only how the stored Midi data is played back. A good example of a common global facility is that of Midi message filtering and remapping:

There are a few occasions when it is useful to be able to restrict the sequencer's recording or use of certain types of Midi messages. Similarly, it's often handy to be able to ask the sequencer to modify certain types of events. The echo-thru option I talked about in chapter 2 is one example of the usefulness of pre-record re-channelling but usually much more can be done... Sequencer One, for instance, has a Set Filter option which allows many other types of Midi messages to be filtered and/or modified. Note on/off, polyphonic aftertouch, program change, pitchbend, and controller information can all be selectively filtered out. It's also possible to convert channel aftertouch messages into controller data, remap controller numbers or even convert controller data into channel aftertouch messages.

Now, at the moment I'll assume that since such things have yet to be mentioned terms like 'controller messages', and therefore these various message remapping (message transformation) facilities, will mean little to you. Don't worry, I'll get around to properly explaining about the various Midi message classes soon. For the moment the important thing is to understand the significance of the fact that these particular Sequencer One facilities are of the 'pre-record' type. If, for example, you decided to set up Sequencer One so that it would filter out program-change messages, any track data subsequently recorded would end up containing no program change messages at all. Any program-change messages that might have been present in the original Midi input stream get lost forever. Most sequencers provide these types of pre-record filter options.

Some sequencers are able to produce filter and conversion effects *after* the data has been stored. These are post-record options and here the effects and settings work on the output side of the sequencer. If you used a post-record filter option to remove program-change messages you would not prevent these messages from being stored in the track or sequence but, even though they ended up being present, any program-change messages would be skipped over when the data was played back.

The big difference of course is that if in the latter scenario you cancelled the program-change filter option, any 'hidden' program-change messages would be brought to life and would again become part of the sequencer's output stream. Post-record options have the benefit of flexibility because you can always undo a particular setting. Pre-record filtering options, however, do still have a use as far as the elimination of the storage of unnecessary information is concerned—which used to be handy on machines where memory was tight. They have become increasingly less attractive as the general editing facilities of commercial sequencers have become more powerful. Most sequencer manuals don't talk about pre-record and post-record effects as such but it is usually obvious from the way that something works what class of editing effect is involved.

Nowadays it is normally feasible to record everything and then decide, retrospectively, what Midi data is to be kept and what data should be discarded. Sequencer One for instance includes facilities for selectively stripping out particular event types from a given track. Again most sequencers offer similar facilities and with some it is possible not only to strip events but to divert those isolated events to another track. Such facilities have taken us well away from the area of global setting-up options and have brought us nicely to another important topic.

At the highest level you can, if you make a mistake whilst you are recording your latest masterpiece, delete the track or sequence and start again - recording, and re-recording, until whatever it is that you are trying to play sounds perfect (or as near perfect as you need it). Sometimes, if you've made a complete hash of it, that's probably the easiest thing to do anyway. Usually things are not quite that bad - you'll find yourself in a situation where most of what you've played sounds fine, but there are one or two places where noticeable slips have been made—a few duff notes or a few bars where the musical timing could have been improved.

Wouldn't it be nice if it were possible to go back and change those bits that weren't quite right? Nowadays you can. And with a sequencer it is actually possible to look at the individual notes in the track or sequence, remove ones that shouldn't be there, add notes that should be there or perhaps alter the pitch or duration of some existing notes.

Having made such changes you just hit the sequencer's Play button and the corrected version will sound the way you wanted it to sound in the first place.

Even relatively short sequences can contain a lot of Midi information and when the status bytes and associated data bytes for each and every sequencer event is shown, the end result can be quite intimidating to the non-technical user. More to the point, the few events which you might be interested in editing can easily get lost amongst the rest of the data. If, for instance, you just wanted to edit or remove a couple of program change events, then having to look through a list containing hundreds of note events (perhaps intermingled with pitchbend and other Midi messages) would make what should be a simple task quite time-consuming. Over the years then it has become apparent that offering the user complete and detailed event lists is not always appropriate.

The key to eliminating the problem of inadvertently providing the user with too much information is simple: Only provide enough event detail to get the job done.

If a user wants to edit program changes events within a track or sequence, then offer them a display which only shows program change messages. If they want to copy and shift around bars of music but are not interested in the detailed contents of those bars, provide a display which allows the track or sequence to be shown as graphical blocks that can be cut-and-pasted around without the user having to see the underlying masses of detailed technical Midi data.

All these ideas have led most sequencer designers to adopt editing schemes which offer high-level graphics based editing as well as low-level, individual event based editing. Bar editors nowadays tend to always be graphics oriented with Midi data being represented as coloured blocks within a track versus bar position framework. Some sequencers provide simple cut-and-paste type facilities for shifting sections of music around, others allow the user to click on a block and view it in more detail or allow the basic block style display to be used for displaying note data, program change data or any other particular Midi event type.

If for instance you wanted to find and edit the program change events within a particular track it might be possible to open a special program change window. With this display all the note data and other non-program-change information would be invisible so finding the one or two coloured blocks which represented program change commands would be very easy. Clicking on the located blocks might then put up a requester showing the current program change value and giving you the opportunity to change it.

With all editors it is usually possible to perform global operations—transpose (change the key of) all the note data within a track for example, or change the Midi channel of the stored data. It is usually also possible to mark a section of that data and perform the same operations on just a limited range of events.

Whilst the basic ideas of information hiding are recognised by all sequencer designers as being both useful and necessary, almost all adopt different approaches to solving the associated problems. Some provide bar and event editing within a single editor, others provide completely separate bar and event editors. Similarly, the sophistication of the editors vary considerably—even within products of similar price ranges.

Cubase provides extremely sophisticated sequence editing facilities.

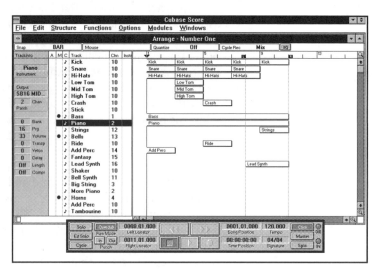

Sequencer One for instance provides a fairly basic bar editor which displays the song as a block graph of track number versus bar contents. Thirty-five bars are shown on the display, and as the song plays the display scrolls so that the currently playing bar is near the centre of the screen. Empty bars are shown as empty (outline) boxes, bars which contain Midi data appear as black boxes. To get more detailed event information Sequencer One provides a separate Step Editor.

Tiger Cub, Dr T's entry level sequencer, provides a rather more sophisticated scheme based around the use of scrollable track and controller windows. Notes are displayed in Tiger Cub as variable size horizontal blocks (whose length represents a note's duration) coupled to vertical velocity stems. Both of these can be directly adjusted graphically with the mouse. Continuous controllers, program changes and so on can be assigned to their own special windows. The emphasis here is on making as much use of graphic-mouse operations as possible.

If for instance you want to create a crescendo—a section in the music where the volume gets gradually louder over a period of time—you can scroll to the appropriate section of music and sketch in a 'volume curve' using the mouse. Full mouse oriented cut-and-paste editing, note drawing, range selection, pitch/velocity/duration editing and note move operations are all extremely easy to carry out. If, you want to move a group of notes you just mark them with the mouse, pick them up and drag them to a new position. Tiger Cub, if you haven't yet realised, is a clever piece of software and its editing facilities have been well designed. Tiger Cub is ideal for users who want a good quality entry level sequencer.

So, what from an editing angle are the other things can you do with a Midi sequencer? The bad news is that even simple sequencers usually have so many different options and facilities that covering every possible editing operation would take a book in itself. Instead I've limited myself primarily to a small selection of topics which for new users are the most important.

*Dr T's Tiger Cub
makes an ideal
entry-level
sequencer for
Amiga users.*

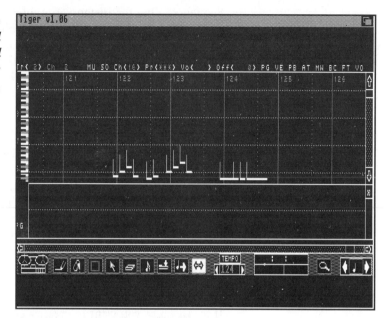

Quantization

When you quantize a track or sequence you ask the sequencer to look at the time positions of the various events and change them so that they fall on well defined time barriers. Supposing, for instance, that you wanted to play a bass line theme which contained four evenly spaced, single beat duration notes per 4/4 bar (what musicians call four crotchets to the bar). You'd pick a suitable tempo, set the sequencer recording, and then play the bass notes.

The chances are that although your timing might be reasonably accurate it is unlikely that it would be 100% perfect. What you could then do is ask the sequencer to globally adjust the note times of the notes present in the track so that, after rounding up or down, they fell *exactly* on the divisions corresponding to the four beats in a 4/4 bar. After you had quantized your bass line track the timing would then be perfect.

Now this is all very well, but there is a snag. Simple quantizing schemes which basically adjust all notes to some user defined time partition (4, 6, 8, 16, 32 ... notes per bar) tend to make the music sound mechanical. It is often the subtle timing and note duration variations in a musicians performance which make it sparkle and sound 'live'. Quantize everything, make it perfect, and the sparkle disappears. There is therefore a very good case for *not* quantizing every piece of Midi data in sight.

Nevertheless, for many Midi users, especially those who have to play keyboards despite the fact that they are not primarily keyboard players, quantization remains an extremely useful facility to have. It is also one of the many sequencer facilities which are becoming more and more powerful because, over the last few years, a lot of effort has gone into finding suitable compromise schemes based on partial quantization. One option is to tidy up the notes a bit without making the timings 100% perfect. Another is to quantize only those notes which lie very near the hypothetical quantize division lines. Some sequencers may offer random improvements so that not all notes are time adjusted by the same amount but all are improved a bit.

Quantization is another facility which tends, as far implementation and use details are concerned, to vary from sequencer to sequencer. Software Technology's Sequencer One allows the beginnings of notes to be quantized whilst keeping the note endings unchanged. Tiger Cub allows the first note in a bar to be fixed (quantize protected) and then allows the quantization of subsequent notes to be made relative to the first note of the bar's time frame. It also allows variable offsets to be added so that a 'swing' feel is introduced to the music. Harmoni (an Amiga sequencer produced by The Disk Company) lets you quantize note start times, note durations, or both. Some sequencers, and Tiger Cub is one example, provide both real-time (pre-record) quantizing and normal edit style quantizing. As you go higher up the scale in sequencer power you find more and more sophisticated quantizing schemes being added.

Software Technology's Sequencer One Plus, which runs on the Atari ST, Atari Falcon and Amiga machines, provides simple yet effective note quantizing schemes. It's another sequencer that is well suited to the newcomer to computers and Midi.

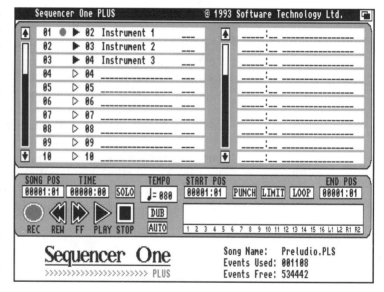

Transposition

Transposition, changing the key of either all or part of a track, is another goodie that comes in very useful at times. If, for example, a piece of music contains a melody that is reused later in different keys, it's possible to paste in copies of the melody at the appropriate positions and transpose them as required.

A lot of musicians use the key of C for all of their keyboard work and then transpose their songs up or down to the required key - it saves having to work out how to play things in different keys. (Most pieces of music are harder to play in some keys than others but the key of C is invariably the easiest.) Believe it or not there are even valid reasons for serious musicians copping out in this admittedly easy fashion. Supposing, for instance, that you are a guitarist or trumpet player who is short of time and interested only in using the synthesizer and sequencer as a convenient way of generating Midi data for creating backing tracks to play along with. You may decide that learning how to play a piano keyboard properly, especially since it's not really the instrument that interests you, is not feasible given the amount of time that you have available.

Automated Voice Selection

I've talked about how multi-track sequencer data can be built up with different Midi channels being used to represent the melodies to be played on different instruments. I also spoke about the relationship between program change messages, synthesizer voices and multiple 'multi-timbral' voice settings. By adding suitable program change events to the sequences that you create it is possible to get the synthesizer to automatically select appropriate voice (or multi-timbral voice) settings.

You might get the impression, since program change messages are transmitted whenever you manually change synthesizer voices, that the easiest way to add a program change command to a sequence is to manually make the change whilst you are recording the track—most synthesizers would sense the change and automatically transmit a program change message. In practice this can work but it is usually easier to insert the program change messages *after* you've done the recording because trying to hit the sequencer's Play/Record button, select a voice and start to play in time on the first beat of a song is usually far from easy!

The exact way that program change messages are added is, like most sequencer operations, invariably sequencer specific. But providing you have worked out what program messages are needed it is always easy to do. Some sequencers just require a number to be inserted in the track list information, some have dedicated menu options, others will require the event to be inserted using the event editor - such things will always be well explained in the sequencer manual.

Sequencer One, for instance, has a Track Info menu item which puts up an information box that, amongst many other things, allows a patch number—a program change number—to be attached to the front of the track. Tiger Cub, Harmoni and Music X also allow these type of initial events to be placed at the start of a sequence.

Most sequencers also allow their event editors to be used to insert program change commands at places other than the start of a track or sequence. Now, you might be asking why one would want to insert a program change command into the middle, or possibly the end, of a sequence. There are several reasons: Firstly you might simply wish to change the synthesizer's voice settings half way through a song. Secondly you may be controlling some other piece of equipment that is turned on when the song starts and is turned off just before the song ends (digital reverb/delay units, which create echo effects, are usually program change controllable).

Re-Channelling

Another useful edit facility, which can normally be applied to either whole sequences or ranged parts of a sequence, is the conversion of data recorded on one Midi channel to a different Midi channel. This, not surprisingly, is called re-channelling. Imagine that a three track piano/violin/bass song has been created using Midi channels 1, 2 and 3 but that the multi-timbral synthesizer setting also has a spare channel (set to Midi channel 4) available but not in use.

Our hypothetical user might decide to make use of the extra channel/voice slot to include a second violin sound, hoping to thicken up, (harmonically enrich) the original violin sound. This is very easy to do and in the above example it would just involve copying the existing Midi channel 2 sequence to a spare sequencer track and then re-channelling the new track so that all channel 2 events were converted to channel 4 events. If the two voices then sounded too similar to be distinguishable some extra editing could be done - a small time delay (usually called a time shift) could be added to one of the tracks, or the second violin track could be transposed up or down an octave. Some sequencers will even let you add small random variations to the note timing so that the second track begins to sound more like a second musician trying to play in unison.

This type of process forms the basis of something called 'sound layering' and it's a trick which has been used in studios for years to improve weak sounding voices (that includes the voices of vocalists as well as instruments). With the Midi sequencer, instrument sound layering can be done with almost no additional effort at all. A complete track can be copied, re-channelled and modified within a couple of seconds and when a separate sound module is being used to generate the layered voice it is possible to use the sequencer's program change editing facilities to step through, and (by playing the sequence) listen to, lots of potential layering voices without ever leaving the sequencer.

In the old days these sorts of tricks were only available in the studio. Only the Rick Wakeman's of the music world (who used to regularly use half a dozen synthesizers at the same time before Midi) could duplicate it live. Nowadays anyone can improve the sound of their synths using these types of voice layering techniques.

You'll find plenty of other edit-oriented descriptions in your own sequencer manuals and these will provide rather more sequencer specific insight into the general issues I've talked about.

5 Drums and Percussion

Percussion, in the musical sense, relates to instruments that are played by hitting them. Percussion instruments therefore include everything from the drums normally found in a drum kit (bass drums, snare drums, cymbals and so on), bongos, tambourines and triangles, right through to the more obscure instruments such as the cabasa and agogo.

Now, I've already talked about the versatility of modern day synthesizers and about the fact that they can be programmed to produce all manner of sounds, including those of the percussion instruments. One might think then that creating a drum accompaniment for a song played on a multi-timbral synth just involves selecting suitable drum sound voices. In fact it isn't quite that straightforward because, set up in the conventional way, a multi-timbral synth would be able play only one voice group setting per channel. Even if you only wanted a bass drum, a snare drum, open and closed hi-hats, a couple of tom-tom drums and a cymbal—which nowadays would be regarded as a very limited drum kit—you'd use up seven Midi channels and a large chunk of your multi-timbral capabilities.

The solution to this potential nasty is to use a slightly different arrangement whereby *all* percussion type note-on/note-off events are sent on just one channel with the note value being used to indicate which particular drum/percussion voice should sound. Some synthesizers and expanders have a special drum channel assigned for this purpose but if you take the hardware that can do this, add some touch-pads which act as drum keys, incorporate memory for storing drum patterns, and finally add some software which permits the creation and editing of all manner of rhythm patterns, you end up with another sort of electronic unit called a drum machine.

Modern drum machines are rather more sophisticated than the above description might suggest. Often they use sampled (digitized) real percussion sounds as opposed to synthesized sounds, the pitch and volume of individual drums voices may be altered, and they usually include loads of preset rhythm patterns which can be used as starting points for building up the drum parts for complete songs. Midi-wise these units will transmit Midi data when they play and the messages transmitted may include start/stop information, Midi timing clocks, and the drum-note data itself. Of course, the reverse procedure can also apply and if the drum machine is sent the appropriate Midi data the drum machine will play the appropriate percussion sounds.

The reason I started by mentioning these drum machines is simple: A great many synthesizers, especially those slightly older models, do *not* have any special drum/percussion facilities. Because of this, depending on which synthesizer you have, you might need a drum machine in order to add drum/percussion sounds to your song arrangements.

Newer synthesizers—especially those such as the Yamaha PSS-590 which are aimed at the lower, mainly non-professional end of the music market—usually do have special built-in drum/percussion facilities. These invariably include a special percussion channel, a set of suitable drum/percussion voices, and preset and user-programmable rhythm patterns. Many such synthesizers include software which can even create the drum accompaniments automatically, although obviously all of these types of facilities are manufacturer dependent. My concern however is not with the use of the built-in accompaniment facilities as such but with the more general themes associated with the recording, editing and playing back of the associated Midi percussion data.

Yamaha produce a range of drum machines including budget priced offerings like this RX8.

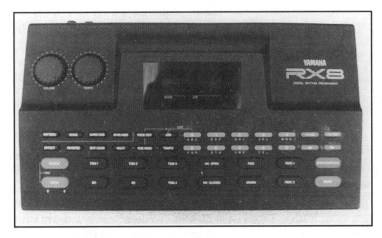

Recording and Playback

As far as the recording and playing back of percussion tracks is concerned it is much the same as recording or playing back ordinary synthesizer data. You can start the rhythm unit playing and record the Midi data that is generated at the Midi Out terminal. But there are a couple of things that you do have to bear in mind: Firstly, you *must not* transpose drum channel data because specific drums and percussion instruments are represented by particular Midi notes - change the note values by transposing them and you'll change the actual percussion voice being played. The effect of inadvertently transposing a drum part will on playback sound disastrous—recorded bass drums might turn into cymbals, the snare drum might vanish and the overall effect is invariably to make the drum/percussion track sound almost unrecognisable.

Obviously it is something that is easily fixed by re-transposing the data back into its original key, thus restoring the original note values.

Some sequencers—Dr T's KCS for instance—allow you to protect a specified Midi channel from transposition. This is convenient because it allows you to carry out all normal editing operations (including transposition) knowing that the note values of the drum/percussion data inside your drum tracks will *not* be altered.

The other thing which needs to be pointed out is that drum machines—or integral synthesizer percussion facilities—vary enormously in the number of different percussion sounds they can provide. Not until fairly recently was there any standardisation between different manufacturers as far as which note numbers would represent which drum sounds. The note which on a Yamaha RX21 drum unit plays a crash cymbal will for instance produce a High Bongo sound on a Roland MT32.

Most companies, however, are at least consistent within the realm of their own products and this, coupled with the fact that the note-to-drum voice correspondences of many percussion units are nowadays user definable anyway, means that most incompatibilities in this particular area are usually easily solved. General Midi, a subject we'll return to in chapter 9, has further helped improve matters.

As far as creating suitable drum patterns is concerned the situation for the beginner is very good indeed because you can cheat! Firstly, you'll be able to use the rhythm patterns and styles available on the percussion unit iself. Secondly, you'll doubtless find that local music stores will stock a number of books which provide details of popular and useful drum patterns written in a block notation style.

Nowadays block notation methods are the most popular notation form, although there is little standardisation in this area. There is no reason of course why, if you have any special needs in this area, you can't develop your own scheme. Since you could even use it to write down your own drum accompaniment ideas it might be useful to go over some typical diagram drum notation.

Block Style Drum Notation

If you saw something like this...

4/4	1	2	3	4	5	6	7	8	9	10	11	12	13	14	15	16
BassDrum																

... it wouldn't take too long to figure out that it had something to do with the bass drum part of a 4/4 bar which needs a resolution—a quantize level that is—of 16 to the bar to represent it.

If you wanted to signify a bass drum playing straight fours to the bar you could therefore do it by marking the appropriate squares...

4/4	1	2	3	4	5	6	7	8	9	10	11	12	13	14	15	16
Bass	●				●				●				●			

By specifying the individual drums needed, and combining all of the drums which are programmed in at a certain quantize level, you could build up a description of a bar like this...

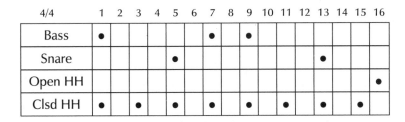

4/4	1	2	3	4	5	6	7	8	9	10	11	12	13	14	15	16
Bass	●					●		●								
Snare				●								●				
Open HH																●
Clsd HH	●		●		●		●		●		●		●		●	

Having a single table is fine when you're dealing with fairly straighforward patterns but if you're including some elements of higher resolution stuff, quantization at 24'ths or 48'ths for triplets in a 4/4 bar say, then the overall table can get a bit unweidly. The best idea then is to make it a rule to use the least resolution possible for any given drum part. In the above example you'd represent the second and fourth snare drum beat using this form...

4/4	1	2	3	4
Snare		●		●

Since with most percussion units you could set the quantize level to 4 in order to enter these snare beats, the breaking up of the diagram in this way makes it easier to do the programming.

The Bass/Snare/Open-HH/Closed-HH example given earlier could therefore be written using these three fragments...

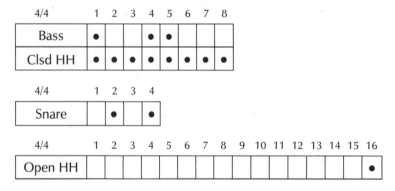

4/4	1	2	3	4	5	6	7	8
Bass	●			●	●			
Clsd HH	●	●	●	●	●	●	●	●

4/4	1	2	3	4
Snare		●		●

4/4	1	2	3	4	5	6	7	8	9	10	11	12	13	14	15	16
Open HH																●

... where each fragment relates to one bar of a 4/4 pattern and uses quantize levels of 8, 4, and 16 respectively.

Accents, which indicate how hard the drums should be hit, can be added to any given drum voice (or voice group) by adding a similar accent strip...

4/4	1	2	3	4	5	6	7	8	9	10	11	12	13	14	15	16
Accent																●
Open HH																●

On drum machines which allow multi-level accents you could even put an accent-level on the diagram using some suitable numerical value written inside the appropriate squares.

There's nothing sacred about the formats I've suggested and they can, and should, be altered as required. The important point to be made is just that these types of schemes are useful because they make it easy to represent drum patterns of almost any complexity. Better than that, the average drum machine will let you program this type of data using an editing mode usually called 'step time'. The name of this step-by-step pattern creation facility itself doesn't matter—what is important is that it makes it possible for anyone to enter the required pattern data.

The result? Beginners (and competent musicians who are non-drummers or non-percussion part readers) can create reasonable sounding rhythm tracks very easily indeed. It is so easy in fact that many Midi musicians let their percussion unit do the whole job for them, but this sort of lazyness has unfortunately led to a myth about drum machines that really should be dispelled.

Boring or What?

It's often said that drum machines tend to produce rather monotonous drum parts. There's no doubt that the average drum machines of a few years ago, with their mediochre sound chips and very limited editing facilities, didn't exactly help stimulate interest in the area of drum programming, but nowadays things have changed and even budget machines like the Yamaha RX8 unit offer good sampled drum sounds which can be tuned, panned, user assigned and generally edited in many ways.

Whilst early drum machines themselves played some role (no pun intended) in the 'monotony syndrome', it was us the users who created the rest of the 'drum-machine's are boring' myth. Part of the problem is that it is all too easy to build a basic pattern and then duplicate it for the duration of the song. Change a few bars, add a couple of extra toms occasionally and bingo... another drum part has been finished. Most musicians have been guilty of that approach at some time or other, especially when pushed for time.

The big question of course is.. what can we do about it? Nowadays, with good percussion units, sequencers and a host of Midi gadgets, there is absolutely no reason at all why you can't create drum parts that are really good. I'm not saying you can build yourself an automated Jeff Porcaro (if you can, write and tell me how) but you can certainly make moves in the right direction.

Let's take things right from scratch: To create interesting drum parts you need a source of inspiration. Whether this comes from you, from ideas picked up by watching others, or from books of examples, doesn't really matter as far as the end results go. Many musicians, especially those who have never sat behind a drum kit, say that their drum programming improved mainly by practice and seeing written examples of interesting drum patterns.

What books are best? That depends on whether you read music or not, but for most people the books which aim to teach you to play a real drum kit are not as useful as those which concentrate solely on offering block notation examples. This, as I've already said, is because the block diagrams in most books are easily programmed into the drum machine, so it is very easy to set up the suggested example patterns.

Music Sales Ltd, who distribute the Amsco Publications books, have a couple of drum-machine books by Rene Pierre Bardet that are worth looking at. One is called '40 Patterns for the Roland Drum Machines' and the other '40 Patterns for the Yamaha, Casio, Korg and Alesis Drum Machines'. Although they are biased towards particular drum machines the patterns themselves are provided in a block form which is easily adapted to virtually all percussion units. You won't, incidentally, need both of them because they deal with similar sets of material - the different formats just make the programming of the different machines easier.

So, assuming (one way or another) that the ideas are there, what else can you do? Mostly it comes down to attention to detail. A common problem is getting the accents right on hi-hat parts. Some accent pads have limited capabilities even though the drum machine is fully velocity sensitive via Midi! In these cases it's usually best to drive it from a touch sensitive keyboard but you'll find, by experimenting, that a lot can also be done by editing the data using your sequencer.

Track Shifting

It's been recognized for some time that if you take a perfectly quantized drum pattern and marginally alter the position of the snare drum—pull it back or push it forwardthat is—then the whole feel of the pattern can change. You can do this sort of thing quite easily via most sequencers simply by recording each drum on a separate track and adjusting the individual start positions.

In theory it all sounds fair enough. In practice there's a minor snag. It is now apparent that quite small differences (even a few milliseconds) can make real contributions to the end result. Why should that be a problem? It's because the Midi clock resolution, which is fixed at 96 clocks per 4/4 bar, cannot resolve or create those sort of very small timing difference effects. Even a tempo of 240 crotchets per minute, which is equivalent to 96 clocks per second, results in an absolute time gap of 10 milliseconds between Midi clocks.

What does that mean in practice? Simply that the Midi clock resolution would enforce a quantize level of at least 10 milliseconds on *any* controllable timing experiment you could do via Midi communications lines. Don't let me put you off experimenting though, because it's still possible to create some good effects. If you really did want to play around with finely tuned delays, you would need a special unit (J L Cooper make one called the FaderMaster). Trouble here is that these 'toys' are fairly expensive and although they do have a number of applications (even in a home Midi-Studio environment) I cannot in all honesty say thay I'd recommend them as essential pieces of Midi equipment.

As well as altering the feel of a drum pattern, track shifting can, when used with the layering technique mentioned in chapter 2, be used to thicken up weak sounding drums. You take the drum track, or a particular part of it, duplicate it onto a second track, shift it along by a small time interval, and play the resulting tracks simultaneously. Done selectively it can be very effective, especially when using hard-left/hard-right stereo panned sound outputs.

Randomisation

Some sequencers will allow you to create randomization masks which will apply a certain amount of modification to a sequence. Again this trick can be used to produce slight non-uniform time-shifts within a quantized sequence. Often the best idea is to duplicate the drum tracks that are to be randomized, then add them back to the original after the magic changes have been made. These sort of tricks do have some disadvantages, not least the fact that duplicate Midi events frequently get inserted into the sequence data. Many sequencer packages (especially the more expensive ones) do in fact provide facilities for removing this type of redundant Midi data.

Using Midi clocks when recording

Someone wrote to me the other day saying that they wanted to use their sequencer to record drum patterns stored in a drum machine. Apparently they were having trouble setting the record speed of their sequencer to the same speed as the drum unit. The result? The attempted recordings of a 24 bar drum part produced sequences which varied from between 23 up to 25 bars in length.

These types of problems are common and occur not just when recording from drum machines but when recording from any external Midi device. Similar sorts of timing problems can occur when you try and link two sequencers together or record complete arrangements from a 'workstation' type synth.

Fortunately the solution is easy. And it also eliminates altogether the need to adjust the sequencer speed to match that of the external Midi device. The trick is to set up the external device so that it generates Midi clocks and then arrange for the sequencer doing the recording to use those clock messages rather than following its own internal timing clock.

Almost all sequencers have menu options for using an external clock in this way. Some also provide controls which allow you to choose whether an explicit Midi Start message is needed to make the sequencer begin recording or whether it should start as soon as the first clock is received. These latter features can be handy when you're dealing with an external Midi device that generates clock data continuously, even when a pattern or sequence is not playing that is. All drum machines, incidentally, do send explicit Midi start messages when a drum pattern begins.

So to record from a drum machine you'd load up your sequencer program and select the external clock option (this is sometimes called 'external sync'). Set the sequencer to record, choose a drum pattern on the drum machine and hit the start button. You'll find that the sequencer will record the pattern exactly, without any bar length timing problems at all.

Now, in case you're wondering how all this works beneath the surface here's a brief run-down on the techie stuff. Midi clocks are single byte Midi messages that have the value decimal 248 (that's F8 hex for any aliens reading). When you set a sequencer to its external clock option the internal timing mechanism is disabled and attention is focused purely on the incoming Midi data.

The external device will be transmitting clock bytes at the rate of 24 per quarter note and these will be received along with all the other Midi data. What happens is that whenever the sequencer reads one of these clocks it adjusts its bar position counter by 1/24th of a quarter note. By the time 24 have been collected the sequencer will know that one bar of data has been received.

When you record data in this way the absolute tempo of the external device doesn't really matter. If you double the playing speed you double the number of Midi clocks sent. Halve it, and you halve the number of Midi clocks. Either way the sequencer will be able to recognise each bar of music as it arrives and if, say, you play exactly 24 bars of a drum pattern you will end up recording exactly 24 bars regardless of tempo.

These type of external clock based Midi links also come in useful on other occasions. You might, for example, have a collection of songs recorded with an old sequencer that didn't provide options for exporting sequences as Midi files. To move those songs across to a more modern sequencer you just need to borrow another computer and link the two machines. It is probably safest for most people to use a Midi connecting lead and two Midi interfaces, but on many machines it can be done by connecting the two computer's serial ports directly using an RS232C cable. Whichever way you choose to connect the hardware, here's what you have to do once you've linked the source and destination machines together and loaded the sequencer program: Set the sequencer that is going to play the song sequences to its internal clock option, making sure that it is also set to generate timing clocks at the same time. Then, set the sequencer being used for recording to its external clock option and start it recording.

Nothing will actually happen until the source sequencer is started. This is because the recording sequencer will be waiting for those all important Midi clocks and these will not appear until the sequencer being used to play the song is actually started. When you do hit the source sequencer's start button, everything should fall into place. The destination (recording) sequencer will record and store the original song material, bar for bar, and there won't be a bar timing glitch in sight!

6 Additional Software and Hardware

Midi is nothing if not versatile, as any trip to a musical equipment show or local music shop will confirm. Sequencers, synthesizers, expanders, drum machines, thru boxes, switchers, mergers, patchbays. In many ways though these things are just the tip of the iceberg and there are plenty of other Midi goodies to be had. On the software front there are notation programs that can be used to create printed scores of your music, some working directly from sequence data. There are patch (voice) editors available that can work directly with the user programmable voice settings held in a synth or expander. Many of these programs provide librarian facilities as well to help you organise your voice data. Early voice editor programs, incidentally, were written for specific use with particular synths or particular synth ranges.

The trend nowadays is to use something called a generic patch editor which will have been designed to work with synthesisers from many different manufacturers. The idea with a generic editor is that, because a broad range of synth products are supported, you will not need to get new editing software when you change your equipment. Dr T's XOR program is a typical example of editing software which uses this approach.

Hardware-wise it is of course the keyboard player who has the most choice as far as Midi equipment goes and this is one good reason why it's useful for everyone involved with Midi to get some keyboard experience. If however you prefer to concentrate your musical attentions in other directions then you'll be pleased to know that all is not lost. There are alternative Midi directions as some of the material in this chapter will show.

Guitarists

There are two areas where a guitarist can use Midi. Firstly, guitar synthesizers, 'Midi guitars', are available that can transmit Midi data as they are played. These let the guitarist who does not want to use the more conventional synthesizer keyboard still get into sequencing and live Midi based playing. Secondly there are Midi controllable amplifiers and effects units that can also be used by the conventional guitarist.

As far as the Midi guitar is concerned, the reason they do not get much music magazine/book coverage is because there are relatively few guitarists actually using them. This doubtless stems from these beasts having a relatively poor track record. Converting conventional sounds into Midi information is a job which, from a technical viewpoint, is far from easy and many snags have been encountered along the development road. Early Midi guitars suffered from so many tracking problems, resulting in wrong notes, notes jumping up and down by a semitone, notes cutting off and so on, that they were virtually unusable outside of a studio.

Guitars, like most stringed instruments, are always prone to tuning problems and so the above Midi difficulties were compounded especially when people tried to convert ordinary guitars to Midi guitars by adding specially designed 'Midi pickup' units. However, the approaches and the technology used have matured over the years and Midi guitars have now improved to the extent where their use to generate Midi data for a sequencer is more than feasible.

But the task of converting a guitar note to an appropriate Midi message is still a relatively difficult job and all Midi guitars take a bit of time to do the necessary conversion. It may only take a tenth of a second or so but the result is that if you expect to be able to pick up a Midi guitar and play fast or do Eddie Van Halen style tricks then you are going to be disappointed. As far as bending notes and playing chords are concerned, however, most Midi guitars can provide resonable performance but you still have to adjust your playing style very much to the guitar rather than expect the Midi guitar to adapt to your particular playing technique. And as far as playing fingerstyle on a Midi guitar goes, you might as well forget it.

The need for playing technique adjustment then is another thing that has limited interest in the Midi guitar. Many guitar purists find this a serious limitation. Not only do they feel uncomfortable about such restrictions but all of the harmonics, flicks, note hammers, vibrato effects and so on—the things that set guitar music apart from that of many other instruments— get lost along the way. At the end of the day the result is that there is little which can be done on the Midi guitar that couldn't be more conveniently done by most musicians with a cheap synth keyboard anyway.

Another snag that is sometimes still encountered is Midi clogging caused because of the enormous amounts of data that can be generated when you bend notes, although most guitar synths do nowadays provide modes which can reduce the amount of bend information transmitted. Basically these limitations are things you have to live with if you want to use a Midi guitar.

To be fair there are benefits as well: Most Midi guitars have conventional pickup circuitry and audio signal output as well as Midi output facilities so the final sounds created by a Midi guitarist can come from the sound modules and synthesizers being driven by the guitar's Midi output, and from the output to a conventional guitar amp. This makes it possible to get excellent 'split sound' effects. If Mono mode is supported you can even have the six strings on six different Midi channels and this means that each string can then be given a different synthesizer voice. Top of the range Midi guitars are expensive.

At the lower end of the scale one company, Casio, did produce a range that were reasonably good although interest from guitarists seemed to be quite limited. Models, such as the Casio MG-510, PG300 and PG 380, can occasionally be found on the second-hand market and picked up extremely cheaply.

Although I've not experienced too many problems with the Midi guitars that I have used, it's only fair to point out that over the years I've heard more than a few Midi-guitar related horror stories. It is always difficult to tell whether snags arise because of real hardware or software faults, incompatibilities between particular combinations of equipment, or just the misfortunes of users new to Midi. As always it is usually safest to err on the side of pessimism and although not always easy to arrange, ideally that means trying the sequencing software and synth equipment with the actual Midi guitar you intend to use.

Effects Unit Control

One use of Midi as far as the guitarists and other instrumentalists are concerned is in controlling devices such as digital delay units, distortion and other effects. There are even a few amplifiers which are Midi controllable. This type of control can be done in two ways: If a sequencer set-up is being used by say the keyboard player of the band or some other instrumentalist, then extra program change events—or whatever else is needed—can just be added to existing sequences to control the additional equipment.

If a sequencer is not available and a musician just wants to control a couple of effects units, or some amplifier settings, then this can be done by using any device that can generate the appropriate Midi control messages. To achieve real-time control like this you need a unit that is convenient to use, and remember here that many musicians' hands are usually fully occupied all the time. There are quite a few add-on foot pedals, like the Digitech PDS3500, that can send the appropriate program change messages or controller messages.

There are also units especially designed with guitarists in mind. One such device, the Datacaster DCT-10/DCR-100, comes from the US-based Lake Butler Sound Company who make all sorts of Midi add-ons. It allows you to send Midi program change commands by using a 10 position switch actually mounted on the guitar itself. The DCR-100, the 'guts' of the device, is a 1U rack-mounting unit which control-wise is a pretty simple affair. The back panel has the power connector and a single Midi Out terminal, the front panel has the rotary click-dial bank and channel switches, the instrument sockets, and an extra input terminal for specialised wireless-link use. At the guitar end you've got to mount the DCT-10, the 10-way control pot, on the guitar. The DC-10 is only a little larger than a normal volume/tone pot and will fit into most existing control areas quite easily.

You could for instance rewire a Strat-style guitar to a master-volume/master-tone configuration and then put the DCT-10 in the unused tone position. The alternative is to fit the DCT-10 as a separate control and here, unless you know what you're doing, the best idea is to have it fitted professionally. The link between the guitar and the DCR-100 unit is via a special Datacaster stereo cable. The benefit of this arrangement is that only one lead is needed between the guitar and the DCR-100 unit, and that carries the audio signal, the power for the DCT-10 switch, and the signals used to trigger the main DCR-100 unit. When you change the switch position on the DCT-10 the main DCR-100 unit is triggered and that in turn generates the appropriate Midi program change message.

The Datacaster is certainly simple to use. You set the channel on the main unit and then select one of the 13 'bank' positions (numbered 0-12). In bank position 0 the guitar control will generate program change messages numbered 0-9, in bank position 1 messages 10-19 are produced, and so on. This means that unless you want to walk over to your rack to change the bank setting you are limited to generating a range of just 10 program change numbers. In the old days this would have been a pain but nowadays, providing the equipment you want to control has a user-assignable program change table, it's not so much of a limitation—unless you are going to need to switch between more than 10 different types of effect. As well as patch selection it's also possible to use the Datacaster in conjunction with other Midi control units.

Foot Controller Boards

Many musicians who want to control effects units on live performances opt for the larger and more versatile footswitch controller boards such as the Boss FC-50. This has six foot controls and four control-change jack-sockets which can be used to sense the state of a number of external pedals/switches, and then generate and transmit the appropriate Midi controller messages. Sockets for two external expression pedals and two footswitches are available and this allows Midi volume information (continuous controller #7), and general purpose continuous controller (#16) messages to be added to the Midi output stream. The two switch type controllers are implemented as the hold controller #64 and a general purpose #80 controller. Recommended FC-50 add-on pedals are the Roland EV5 and the Boss EV10.

A controller board like the FC-50 can therefore allow musicians to remotely select particular settings or 'programs' without the need to make manual changes to the front panel controls of their Midi equipment. The latest generation of foot controller boards are tending to put increasingly more facilties on board. Philip Rees MM5 programmable foot controller for example provides mapping facilities, sysex uploading and downloading of settings, and can act as a Midi clock source. It also provides auto-accompaniment, harmonisation and transposition facilities as well as conventional program and control change data.

The Philip Rees MM5 programmable foot controller.

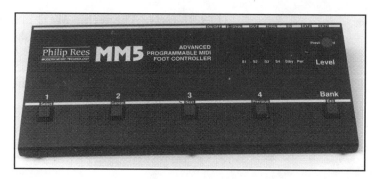

Midi Filters

Message filtering is the removing of unwanted Midi messages and this is usually done when sequences are first created. There are occasions however, particularly for live performances involving some types of very old Midi equipment, where filter boxes inserted into a Midi line have proved useful. A number of companies therefore produced boxes that provide selective filtering of various message types—Midi clocks, controllers, pitchbend, program change commands, messages associated with particular channels and so on. As both sequencers and Midi equipment in general have become more flexible there's no doubt that the demand for these types of separate filter devices has fallen, although they are still available.

SMPTE/TimeCode Applications

One way of synchronising a sequencer to a multitrack tape recorder is to use a box that converts Midi clock messages sent from the sequencer into a tone which is recorded on tape. On playback this tone is converted back into Midi clocks. These frequency shift keying (FSK) systems are relatively cheap but they do have a number of disadvantages. A better arrangement, and the one used by professional users involves something called SMPTE. Although this area is really outside this scope of this book, here are a few introductory notes.

WARNING: The techie MTC message descriptions in the following sections have been provided for more advanced Midi users and have been included here simply because this is the only area of the book which deals with SMPTE/TimeCode. Most readers may prefer to ignore the technical descriptions on first reading.

SMPTE is a Sound Motion Picture and Television Engineer's standard for an audio signal used to encode timing information. Time stamps are represented in terms of a time of day (hours, minutes, seconds and 'frames') which can be recorded onto an audio or video tape and then used to synchronise other devices, 'lock' them, that is, to that same time frame. SMPTE can keep other units in sync with tape devices even if there are minor fluctuations in tape speed, and since it can be read both forwards and backwards it is an ideal way of synchronising Midi sequencing equipment to tape.

Units which write SMPTE data produce an audio type signal which can be recorded on one track of a multi-track tape recording machine. On playback, fast forward or rewind operations the track containing the SMPTE stripe will be read by the SMPTE sync unit and this enables the tape position to be identified either during or after any amount of tape movement. Now this is all very well. You have the SMPTE unit sitting between your Midi/computer gear and the tape-recorder generating and reading the appropriate SMPTE info, but this will only provide the tape-to-sync-box communications connection. The sequencer—or whatever package is running—needs to be given that same time stamp information. There are two basic approaches.

One solution is to provide direct computer-to-sync-box hardware links. This is done with units like Dr T's Phantom interface. Another way to lock computerised Midi gear into this SMPTE time frame is to use Midi Time code (MTC). This is the Midi message equivalent of the SMPTE time frame standard and these messages are a relatively new addition to the Midi standard. There are actually three message variants but from the real-time SMPTE user's viewpoint the form that is most important is called the Quarter Frame Message. This is a two byte System Common Midi message which adopts the format shown in figure 6.1.

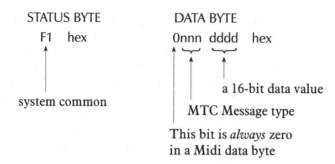

Figure 6.1: Internal layout of a Quarter Frame Midi Time Code message.

The Quarter Frame message can hold eight different types of time info. As you'll see from Figure 6.1 the seven bits of data held in a quarter frame MTC message is split into two parts. The three bits which identify the time data contained in the message use this sort of encoding scheme...

nnn	*message type*	
0	Frame count	least significant four bits
1	Frame count	most significant four bits
2	Seconds count	east significant four bits
3	Seconds count	most significant four bits
4	Minutes count	least significant four bits
5	Minutes count	most significant four bits
6	Hours count	least significant four bits
7	Hours count	most significant four bits

To send a complete SMPTE time data description all eight of the above message subtypes need to be transmitted, so these MTC messages should really be thought of as occurring in groups of eight.

When a SMPTE sync box is reading timecode info and generating Midi Time Code messages at normal playing speed it will be transmitting this type of information continuously. During fast-forward or rewind however what usually happens is that the sync unit will usually wait until the tape stops and then transmit a message giving the final SMPTE position. Some units do send the occasional MTC position update messages.

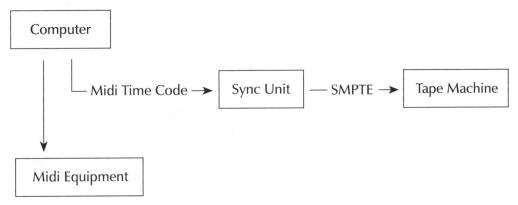

Figure 6.2: The SMPTE-MTC time frame communication scheme.

The computer-to-tape connection is therefore built up of two parts, both of which rely on the SMPTE time stamp standard. Real SMPTE code handles the tape-to-SMPTE sync unit part of the story, and Midi Time Code handles the SMPTE sync unit-to-computer link. Nowadays it usually all fits together quite well. There are four variants of SMPTE code but even the fastest real-time data—which time stamps at 30 frames per second—is easily handled. In fact MTC requires less than 8% of the Midi bandwidth for its data, which means its use produces a loading of less than 8% of the full capacity of a Midi line when transmitting messages at its maximum possible rate.

Having said that I'd be less than honest if I said that MTC related Midi problems do not exist. There is actually an awful lot more to the SMPTE/MTC story and programming-wise it gets quite complicated. Variations in interpretations of the Midi standard, and in the extent (or the lack) of MTC support will obviously directly affect the success of such applications program SMPTE/MTC links. It is usually best to see any SMPTE/MTC unit actually running with your chosen Midi software before buying!

Those other MTC messages? Although the Quarter Frame messages handle the bulk of the real-time work they are not always suitable. In cases where a lot of fast-forwarding, rewinding and cueing operations are being done the Midi standard provides a special Full Time Code message that can be sandwiched inside a conventional system exclusive message. Another sysex-oriented MTC message, which is intended mainly for professional users, allows for special User Bit information.User Bit data consists of 32 bits of application specific data that is used for encoding things like tape-reel numbers and other hardware/device specific header info.

Wireless Midi

One way of eliminating the 15 metre Midi cable length restriction is to use a wireless (radio) link, and these are available from a number of sources. I have only ever used one wireless Midi system and this proved both unreliable for live work and unusable for handling heavy, sequencer based Midi traffic, which ruled it out for studio use. I would stress however that the system I tried was an early one and I'm not going to name the company because their system may well have improved by now. There are a number of radio and infra-red based systems aimed at the professional marketplace, but these are expensive and have limited applications anyway.

Specialist Midi Cables

There are a number of alternative ways of breaking the 15 metre Midi cable length limit, including fibre optic based Midi cable links and the use of line driver units which convert the Midi signals into a form suitable for long distance cable transmission. Some systems can work at distances of 1000 metres or so and since these extended length cable systems are intended for professional use they are normally designed to work reliably in electronically 'noisy' environments. Theatre companies, recording studios, PA hire companies and the like will use these types of cables for remotely controlling on-stage effects, lighting and so on.

One of the first line driver units to appear came from a company called Philip Rees who produced a Midi Line Driver (MLD) system which allowed Midi signals traverse up to a kilometre. The original MLD system was unidirectional, but in some installations bidirectional Midi communication is required, or control is needed where there is no readily available source of power at the remote end. The latest units to help in this area again come from Philip Rees and are called MTR Midi Line Transmitter/Receiver boxes. They allow cable runs of up to 150 metres to be used and consist of a pair of units with the cable link between each unit being made either with screened twisted pair cables or, as is more common in professional applications, by incorporating the devices into paths that end up being sent down multicore cable.

With the MTR system only one unit is mains-powered. This 'master transceiver' has power, Midi In, Midi Out and Line connectors, plus an indicator LED to let you know that the unit is powered-up. The second, remote slave transceiver derives its power from the line itself and so has only the Midi In, Midi Out and Line connectors.

Because the MTR can work down multicore you'll often find MTR based control systems installed in theatres to control lighting or to trigger stage effects. There are plenty of other situations where the ability to get Midi data down long cable runs is equally important. In recording studios, particularly with remotely located control rooms, an MTR system can be part of the permanent installation. They can also be used on an ad hoc basis, with the remote unit employed rather like a DI box.

Philip Reees MLD line drivers are one of a number of products which allow very long Midi cable lengths to be used.

Lighting and Other Midi Control Applications

Ever since Midi arrived on the scene manufacturers and developers realised that as well as its pure musical applications Midi had the potential for control of all manner of electrical equipment. Those who formulated the standard did after all include a whole range of switch and continuous controller commands as well as a sysex (system exclusive) message packet for the more esoteric needs of developers. Whilst modern computers can obviously provide a highly cost-effective brain for any control switching application it is not always necessary to have access to a computer based sequencer in order to generate Midi control data.

Nowadays a whole range of programmable controllers and foot pedal boards are available for generating note, controller, sysex or any other kind of Midi data.

In the main it has understandably been the manufacturers of Midi synthesizers, expanders and sound effect units that have made the most use of Midi control functions, although in recent years a number of other areas of use have developed. Rack mounted Midi controlled patchbays are available which allow recording studios and stage production companies to remotely control audio signal routing and so on. Whilst the more sophisticated patchbay units are expensive, a number of companies do produce simpler switching units. U.S. based Midi Solutions for example, as well as providing plenty of thru/merge and filter units, also offer a Midi controlled relay switch. Whilst these are most often used for controlling punch-in on multi-track tape machines, a variety of other uses, like controlling a camera being used for time-lapse still photography, can be envisaged.

One switching applications area that has taken off in recent years is Midi controlled light switching. A variety of units are available and they are used for everything from stage show and department store window lighting displays to club disco/dance lighting uses. One unit that is available for semi-pro (low wattage) use comes from BCK Products and is called the Lite Show. This provides eight 300 watt outputs which can be programmably switched and faded using Midi channel 16. Fixed but custom channel modifications can be made to order if required.

The Lite Show responds to three types of Midi message: Note on messages, program change commands and active sensing. It's the note on messages that control the lights, with Midi notes 60-67 selecting the lighting channel and the velocity byte of each message determining the brightness. Program change messages are used to switch between one of 65 preset and 15 dynamically changing 'super scene' settings.

One of the things that those of you who are already Midi -literate are bound to have noticed is that the Lite Show commands have been implemented using note on messages rather than continuous controller messages as might be expected. This is often the case with such units, and the reason quite simply is that a continuous controller scheme is harder and more expensive to implement.

Another lighting control product that has become very popular amongst professional users is the Profile Music MP820 switcher. This provides eight channels with a power rating of over 1000 watts per channel and with this device both the Midi channel, and the range of notes to which the unit responds, are user selectable. The MP820 again uses a note/velocity based light control scheme but in addition to this Midi continuous controller #96 has been implemented to allow fade and delay characteristics to be changed under Midi control.

For professional users Profile Music offer a rack mounted expansion unit which allows banks of MP820s to be linked, providing up to 2,048 lighting channels—and potentially over two megawatts of lighting control! The same company also have Midi/DMX controllers and Midi controlled laser products currently under development.

Midi to DIN Sync Conversion

Another control area that, though musical, did ought to be mentioned. This is the use of Midi in controlling older, non-Midi, types of percussion and arpeggiator equipment. The Midi standard includes a group of single-byte commands called the System Real Time (SRT) messages, four of which are concerned with equipment synchronisation—Clock, Start, Continue and Stop. Some older equipment, however, requires an older form of synchronisation control, something called the Sync24 system which was introduced by Roland many years ago and subsequently adopted by several other manufacturers.

Sync24 is popularly known as 'DIN Sync', because it uses the round 5-pin DIN connector, coincidentally the same as is used for Midi. Although the same type of connectors are used, you should never directly connect Midi sockets to Sync24 sockets because the two systems are totally incompatible. In fact, if it is necessary to control older types of Sync 24 based equipment via Midi, a special converter needs to be used. One such unit, the MDS Midi To Sync 24 Converter, is now available from Philip Rees. The unit listens to an incoming Midi SRT clock stream and generates a corresponding DIN sync format output. The result is that Sync24 devices can be started, will play in time, and be stopped automatically, by sending conventional real time Midi messages from your sequencer or master keyboard.

Still Only Scratching the Surface

As well as the well known Midi gadget manufacturers like J.L. Cooper, Midi Solutions, Philip Rees and so on, there are numerous more specialised companies that build customised Midi control units for professional users. Such companies can provide things like fibre optic Midi cable links, wireless based Midi links and so on but needless to say the cost of these types of esoteric solutions puts them out of reach of the average Midi user. Although not in wide use outside of professional circles, a number of mixer units are available nowadays that store fader adjustments in memory locations that can be called up by program change messages.

Whatever hardware is involved, obviously the most control flexibility is obtained by using a sequencer to initially store the appropriate Midi message information. Once a control sequence has been prepared, however, it is perfectly feasable to save the sequence as a Midi file and then, say, use a standalone Midi file player for playing the programmed sequence of control changes. For example a department store lighting display could be driven in this way very easily indeed, and with these 'control oriented' application areas Midi equipment suppliers are really only just beginning to realise the potential.

Plenty of golden opportunities for entrepreneurs with the right mix of drive and ingenuity exist, not only to push the limits of Midi even further but also to make a few bucks for themselves along the way!

7 Midi Implementation Charts

In earlier chapters I've talked about buying synthesizers and explained a little of what they can do. One of the things that should have become apparent is that synthesizers, and all other types of Midi equipment come to that, can vary enormously in the facilities they provide. I'm not just talking about sound quality and construction, which obviously tend to improve as the price of the instrument increases, I'm talking about the capabilities that the various instruments have for sending, receiving and understanding the various classes of Midi messages that have been defined. Strange as it may seem the Midi standard itself does not specify exactly what transmission/reception facilities particular pieces of equipment should have - such things are left up to the manufacturer.

Because of this it helps to know before you buy a piece of equipment which Midi functions are supported and which are not.

The Midi Implementation Chart is a way of presenting this information in a concise and standardised form. You will find these charts in the instruction manuals of almost every piece of Midi equipment on the market, so it is well worthwhile learning how to understand them. A Midi Implementation Chart is a standardised table which details the Midi function names, indicates the transmission and reception characteristics of the equipment, and provides additional remarks which help in the chart interpretation.

The basic layout, with some of the fields labelled to help with the explanations, is shown in Figure 7.1.

Type of Product				
Model			Chart Date / Version	
Midi Function		Transmitted	Recognised	Remarks
Basic Channel	Default			
	Changed			
Mode	Default			
	Messages			
	Altered			
Note Number				
	True voice			
Velocity	Note ON			
	Note OFF			
Aftertouch	Key			
	Channel			
Pitchblend				
Control Change				
Program Change				
	#True			
System Ex.				
System Common	Song Pos Pointer			
	Song Select			
	Tune			
System RT	Clock			
	Commands			
Aux Messages	Local ON/OFF			
	All Notes OFF			
	Active Sensing			
	Reset			
Notes				

(Letters down the left margin: A, B, C, D, E, F, G, H, I, J, K, L, M, N, O, P, Q, R, S, T, U, V, W, X, Y, Z)

Figure 7.1: General Midi Implementation Chart Layout.

At the top of the chart there are details of the type of product, the model name, and the preparation date and version number. Following this the chart divides into four columns (line label A) with the first column providing the names of the various classes of Midi messages. The data in the next column shows the transmission characteristics of the unit; in other words it tells you the types of messages that the unit can send to other units. The third column does the reverse, it shows which types of Midi messages can be understood by the equipment. The column on the far right is used for general remarks and additional technical notes.

Once you have a fair idea of what the various classes of Midi messages are used for you'll find that most of the data provided in the four implementation chart columns will be self-explanatory. For the moment though, here are a few notes to help.

Field B holds the default Midi channel number. If this channel number can be memorized (stored when the unit is switched off) then this will be shown in the remarks column. Field C shows whether it is possible to change the basic channel number of the equipment and field D specifies the default Midi mode, the 'power up' mode state. Field E identifies the mode messages which can be sent and understood by the equipment, with the next line, field F, identifying the mode selected if the unit receives a mode message that it cannot understand.

The range of Midi note numbers that can be transmitted and received is shown in field G. Often the reception range is wider than the range of notes which can actually be played by the instrument. What usually happens is that notes at the extremes are automatically transposed up or down until they fall within the note range that the unit can cope with. Field H shows the pitch range of the notes that will sound in terms of the Midi note numbers.

Touch response information, velocity data that is, is shown in Field I and here you should remember that just because a synthesizer does not have a touch-sensitive keyboard—and hence cannot transmit key pressure related velocity data—it does not necessarily mean that the synth cannot understand such data when it is provided from another source. You will find that most non touch-sensitive keyboards are able to use incoming velocity information. Field J is used to provide details of a unit's note off velocity characteristics.

In addition to note-on and note-off velocity data, many touch-sensitive keyboards will be able to transmit aftertouch information. Fields K and L provide the details, and again you'll find quite a few non touch-sensitive synthesizers that are able to use aftertouch messages sent from another source.

Field M tells you whether pitch bend information can be transmitted or recognized, and immediately after this you'll find a table—shown as Field N—that gives controller numbers and their designated effects. If program change messages can be sent or recognized, this will be indicated in the appropriate columns of Fields O and P. Similarly, Field Q provides summary details of any sysex capabilities. For full sysex details you will need to delve into the appropriate sections of the main manual.

The next three fields (R, S and T) show whether song pointer messages can be transmitted or recognized, whether song select messages can be sent or recognized, or if the unit can send or respond to a tune request. In all cases, if a facility is supported then you'll find 'yes' entries present in the appropriate columns.

Fields U and V tell you about any real-time message capabilities. They will show whether Midi timing clock messages can be sent or recognized and whether start, continue or stop commands are transmitted or understood. The following four fields (W, X, Y and Z) show whether local on/off, all notes off, active sensing or system reset messages are supported. If, for example, the all notes off message is understood by the unit you'll find details in the Recognized column.

Lastly comes some space where the manufacturer can write anything. Most use this space to provide qualifying information which assists in the interpretation of data given earlier.

So that's what you'll find in a Midi implementation chart and the good news is that the charts for *all* equipment will use this standardised form. The benefit is that not only do prospective buyers of a piece of equipment get a chance to see a summary of the type of Midi facilities which the equipment provides, but they get the summary in a form which makes it easy to compare different offerings. It's little wonder that when buying new equipment most experienced Midi users ask to see the manual—what they do of course is turn straight to the page which gives the implementation chart, and then use that as their initial guide to the instrument.

8 Midi Fault Finding

Almost everyone meets the odd Midi snag at one time or another. You connect your equipment, switch on and bingo—it either doesn't work as expected or it doesn't work at all!

What could be wrong?

If the sequencer isn't recording it could be incorrectly set up. Alternatively, the synthesizer which is feeding the sequencer could have been set up badly, or a lead may be faulty. In more unfortunate cases there may actually be a hardware fault on your computer or on one or more pieces of Midi equipment.

A lot of problems are easily resolved.

Perhaps you are transmitting program change messages, or transmitting control sequences, and they do not seem to be having the right—or any—effect? This will often be simply because the receiving equipment is set to a different Midi channel. It's rarely difficult to plan suitable courses of fault-finding actions in such cases:

Ask yourself what faults could fit the known facts, and then try to find ways of eliminating each fault from your investigations. If you tackle these things from the data source and trace your way along in a logical fashion, it usually doesn't take more than a few minutes to come up with the right answers.

For sequencer transmitted data you might start at the computer end of the set-up and ask yourself how you tell whether the computer is transmitting anything. An indicator light can provide a useful clue. Perhaps your synth has a light which flashes as data is received?

As with most things, a bit of commonsense goes a long way and it does of course pay to start by considering those things which, from past experience, seem likely candidates. If, for example, you have four Midi units chained together and being driven by a sequencer, yet only the first one of them appears to be receiving any Midi signals, then you ought to realize that there is a good chance that the cause is related to the lead between the first and second Midi units.

As fault-finder your first instinct should be to check the connections between the first two Midi units and make sure that not only have the correct Midi sockets been used but that the connectors have been properly pushed in. Once satisfied that no silly slips in these areas have been made you might consider that the lead between those first two units is to blame. Look at the DIN connectors. Dirt and grime could possibly create a poor contact, and although this is not particularly likely it is an easy and quick check to make.

If the connectors on the lead look OK, then having eliminated other likely alternatives you should be led to the conclusion that there is at least a high probability of the lead having an internal break somewhere. A reasonable next step would therefore be to swap that suspect lead for another one. The object of the exercise now being to attempt to either prove by eliminating the fault that the connecting lead was to blame, or to disprove it by showing that changing leads made no difference.

These types of commonsense-driven arguments will usually lead you to the right conclusions very quickly but it is important to realize that you should always go for the obvious potential causes first: Unlikely possibilities, such as there being a hardware fault in the second unit, should not be considered until the more likely things have been checked. Rank outsiders, such as there being three separate cases of hardware faults, should not really be entering your mind during early investigations!

Sometimes, however, the problem may not be quite so easily solved and in cases where you are finding it difficult to tell what Midi messages are actually being sent down the line it may even help to get away from your sequencer and generate the equivalent messages using your own diagnostic or Midi utility programs.

There are many occasions where home-grown Midi programs can be of use; programs which can generate program change messages, Midi time clocks, or short sysex messages frequently come in handy. Similarly, a program which can read incoming Midi data and tell you about the types of messages which are arriving can be used to good effect. All of these things, if you have a little programming experience, are quite easy to do, but rather than clutter this general fault finding chapter with technical programming details I've reserved this rather specialised area for Chapter 15 and some appendices. Diagnostic software, incidentally, cannot solve all Midi fault finding problems.

The trouble is, of course, that you cannot use your computer/sequencer as a diagnostic tool whilst at the same time using it as a sequencer. Often you'll need to have the sequencer running in order to generate the Midi data that is causing the problem in the first place. You could get another computer, but a far cheaper solution is to get a separate Midi diagnostic device that can be used at the same time as your sequencer.

The StudioMaster MA36 Midi Analyser

The diagnostic device that I use is called the MA36 and it is made by a company called StudioMaster, best known for their audio mixing desks. The MA36 is not a new device but it is still not particularly well known outside of serious Midi circles. From the letters I get about Midi fault finding it is obvious that there are a lot of Midi users who could benefit from an MA36 and I can tell you quite truthfully that I've been using my unit almost daily for years to tackle all kinds of Midi problems. It is as invaluable today as it was when I first bought it and if, as a new Midi user, you were to ask me what I considered the most important first Midi extra to add to a basic Midi set up I would say an MA36 analyser.

After an introduction like that you should rightly be curious about this gadget, so here are some details. The MA36 measures about 7 cm x 12 cm x 3 cm, has an on/off switch, can be battery or mains-adapter powered and has two Midi sockets, namely Midi In and Midi Thru. As Midi data passes through the unit the MA36 identifies the messages and displays the results on a set of LEDs situated on its front-panel. The right-hand side of the MA36 display is a bank of channel indicators. These enable you to tell immediately what Midi channels are being used. The left-hand side of the display provides details of the message types being received, so if for instance you want to know whether the Midi data that is supposed to be coming into your synthesizer is really there, you just take the lead out of your synthesizer's Midi In terminal and plug it into the MA36.

If the data is there you'll instantly see what messages are being transmitted, plus any associated channel numbers. There is very little else one can say about the MA36 except that it is one of those delightful little boxes that you don't need to be a genius to use.

StudioMaster's MA36 Midi Analyser unit.

Hand-held Midi Message Transmitter Units

Another extra that can sometimes be of use is a portable unit which can generate Midi messages. A number of companies make such units and one that I have used frequently is the ForeFront Technology's FT3 patch commander. It is a hand held, battery powered unit intended for use as a general Midi remote controller, and it has nine different modes of operation. The FT3 will function as a patch command transmitter which can transmit a patch message on any or all Midi channels. Eight such settings can be stored so that they can be recalled using a single keypress; this data is retained when unit is switched off.

There are system and channel filter modes which enable you to filter unwanted Midi messages from your Midi data. You can even use the FT3 to switch running status on or off. Data sent using running status can therefore have the status bytes re-inserted into the Midi stream) The FT3 also includes a Midi clock generator and a Midi lead tester.

Forefront Technology's FT3 Patch Commander.

9 General Midi and Roland GS

The standardisation offered by Midi has opened up a wealth of musical possibilities. But despite the fact that instruments from different manufacturers can be linked very easily, there are some recognised problem areas. One is the relationship between the sounds that you hear on one particular synth or sound module (plus the commands or voice-memory-slots that are related to them), and the equivalent characteristics on another manufacturers unit.

Midi notes are timbreless, that is they're not specifically related to any particular sound or synthesizer voice. In many ways this is good because it offers a lot of flexibility. You can for instance record a melody with your synthesizer set up for a flute sound but if, before playing it back, you change the synthesizer's voice to say a piano sound then the melody you recorded will play back sounding like a piano. Such changes can even be done by remote control by getting the sequencer to transmit program-change (patch-selection) messages.

Program change numbers as originally envisaged by the committee that formulated the Midi spec had nothing directly to do with the various audible sounds that a synthesizer can make. In fact, given the infinitely wide range of sounds that all synthesizers can produce, plus the fact that many voice settings would be user-programmable anyway, it was not originally felt to be feasible to implement any scheme which associated given program change numbers with particular types of sound.

Manufacturers, then, were rather left to their own devices as far as the program change-to-voice correspondence was concerned. The result, as most Midi users will be only too painfully aware, is an annoying situation where a program change #70 message might select a flute voice on one synthesizer, yet the same message sent to another synthesizer might select an accordion sound.

There are other problems. The lack of drum-voice and drum-note standardisation makes life equally awkward on the percussion front, and re-editing sequence data so that it conforms to alternative voice, channel and drum-note arrangements can be quite a job even for the expert Midi user. When it comes to using other people's sequences there are problems to be found with polyphony. What happens, for instance, if a 12-note polyphonic expander is given more than 12 notes to play at a time?

So there are problems with controller standardisation.

As far as reconfiguring new pieces of equipment to suit existing patch/voice assignments, most synths and modules are reasonably flexible. So for the lone Midi user working mainly with their own sequence data these types of snags are not the end of the world. The difficulties increase when you start to use lots of sequences created by other people: It is simply not practical to keep changing the equipment voice-configurations each time you wish to use someone else's sequence data. And it certainly isn't reasonable to assume that everyone has synths and sound modules with infinitely re-assignable controllers and unlimited polyphony.

These particular areas of difficulty were identified some time ago, with many companies realising that the lack of standardisation in this area was holding back the formation of a large pre-recorded sequenced music market. Apart from the obvious things like 'music minus-one' type songs (backing sequences where you just add the melody), and Midi versions of instrumental music, there are a number of other areas to be explored: Imagine having song sequence data in a form that was so standardised that you'd be able to play it on your Midi equipment in much the same way as you'd play a CD, not having to worry about what equipment it was actually recorded on or what types of controller and program change messages were being used!

It is this general consumer market, rather than inherent concern for the poor musician, that has prompted interest from the manufacturers of Midi equipment. This non-musician based Midi market is potentially massive. It includes things like computer game music, CD+Midi media formats, music educational and business presentation software, and integrated audio-visual (AV) equipment. Those types of applications mean big bucks and since it was the lack of generally acceptable voice/patch and drum note standardisation that seemed to be holding things back it was hardly surprising that much effort has gone into finding a solution.

What is it? General Midi (GM). Instruments that are GM compatible have certain characteristics. They recognise channel aftertouch, pitchbend, mod-wheel, volume, pan, expression and sustain controllers, plus they have a minimum of 24 voices simultaneously available, including eight for drums. Program change commands select from a pre-defined voice set which is based on the sounds shown in Table 9.1. Percussion instruments use a standardised drum map on Midi channel 10 (Table 9.2).

Voice Number	Voice Name	Voice Number	Voice Name
(Piano)		(Lead)	
1	Acoustic Piano 1	65	Soprano Sax
2	Acoustic Piano 2	66	Alto Sax
3	Acoustic Piano 3	67	Tenor Sax
4	Honky Tonk Piano	68	Baritone Sax
5	Electric Piano 1	69	Oboe
6	Electric Piano 2	70	English Horn
7	Harpsichord	71	Bassoon
8	Clavinet	72	Clarinet
(Chromatic Percussion)		(Pipe)	
9	Celesta	73	Piccolo
10	Glockenspiel	74	Flute
11	Music Box	75	Recorder
12	Vibraphone	76	Pan Flute
13	Marimba	77	Bottle Blow
14	Xylophone	78	Shakuhachi
15	Tubular Bell	79	Whistle
16	Santur	80	Ocarina
(Organ)		(Synth Lead)	
17	Organ 1	81	Square Wave
18	Organ 2	82	Saw Wave
19	Organ 3	83	Synth Calliope
20	Church Organ 1	84	Chiffer Lead
21	Reed Organ	85	Charang
22	Accordion Fr	86	Solo Vox
23	Harmonica	87	5th Saw Wave
24	Bandneon	88	Bass & Lead

(Guitar)		(Synth Pad. Etc)	
25	Nylon String Gtr	89	Fantasia
26	Steel String Gtr	90	Warm Pad
27	Jazz Gtr	91	Polysynth
28	Clean Gtr	92	Space Voice
29	Muted Gtr	93	Bowed Glass
30	Overdrive Gtr	94	Metal Pro
31	Distortion Gtr	95	Halo Pad
32	Guitar Harmonics	96	Sweep Pad

(Bass)		(Synth SFX)	
33	Acoustic Bass	97	Ice Rain
34	Fingered Bass	98	Soundtrack
35	Picked Bass	99	Crystal
36	Fretless Bass	100	Atmosphere
37	Slap Bass 1	101	Brightness
38	Slap Bass 2	102	Goblin
39	Synth Bass 1	103	Echo Drops
40	Synth Bass 2	104	Star Theme

(Strings/Orchestra)		(Ethnic)	
41	Violin	105	Sitar
42	Viola	106	Banjo
43	Cello	107	Shamisen
44	ContraBass	108	Koto
45	Tremolo Strings	109	Kalimba
46	Pizzicato Strings	110	Bag Pipe
47	Harp	111	Fiddle
48	Timpani	112	Shanai

(Ensemble)		(Percussive)	
49	Strings	113	Tinkle Bell
50	Slow String	114	Agogo
51	Syn Strings 1	115	Steel Drums
52	Syn Strings 2	116	Woodblock
53	Choir Aahs	117	Taiko
54	Voice Oohs	118	Melo Tom 1
55	Syn Vox	119	Synth Drum
56	Orchestra Hit	120	Reverse Cymbal
(Brass)		(SFX)	
57	Trumpet	121	Guitar Fret Noise
58	Trombone	122	Fl. Key Click
59	Tuba	123	Seashore
60	Muted Trumpet	124	Bird
61	French Horn	125	Telephone 1
62	Brass 1	126	Helicopter
63	Synth Brass 1	127	Applause
64	Synth Brass 2	128	Gun Shot

Table 9.1: The General Midi Instrument Sound Set.

Note	*ToneName*	*Name*
B1	(35)	Kick Drum 2
C2	(36)	Kick Drum 1
C#2	(37)	Side Stick
D2	(38)	Snare Drum 1
D#2	(39)	Hand Clap
E2	(40)	Snare Drum 2
F2	(41)	Low Tom 2
F#2	(42)	Closed Hi-Hat
G2	(43)	Low Tom 1
G#2	(44)	Pedal Hi-Hat
A2	(45)	Mid Tom 2
A#2	(46)	Open Hi-Hat
B2	(47)	Mid Tom 1
C3	(48)	High Tom 2
C#3	(49)	Crash Cymbal 1
D3	(50)	High Tom 1
D#3	(51)	Ride Cymbal 1
E3	(52)	China Cymbal
F3	(53)	Ride (on Bell)
F#3	(54)	Tambourine
G3	(55)	Splash Cymbal
G#3	(56)	Cowbell
A3	(57)	Crash Cymbal 2
A#3	(58)	Vibraslap
B3	(59)	Ride Cymbal 2
C4	(60)	High Bongo
C#4	(61)	Low Bongo
D4	(62)	Mute High Conga
D#4	(63)	Open High Conga
E4	(64)	Low Conga
F4	(65)	High Timbale
F#4	(66)	Low Timbale

G4	(67)	High Agogo
G#4	(68)	Low Agogo
A4	(69)	Cabasa
A#4	(70)	Maracas
B4	(71)	Short Whistle
C5	(72)	Long Whistle
C#5	(73)	Short Guiro
D5	(74)	Long Guiro
D#5	(75)	Claves
E5	(76)	High Wood Block
F5	(77)	Low Wood Block
F#5	(78)	Mute Cuica
G5	(79)	Open Cuica
G#5	(80)	Mute Triangle
A5	(81)	Open Triangle

Table 9.2 The General Midi Percussion Map.

The Roland GS Standard

Roland GS standard takes these General Midi' ideas much further. For compatibility with GM the standard specifies a tone map which defines the basic instrument tones along with assigned program change numbers. The program change ideas have been expanded so that sounds (voices) can be defined on a two-dimensional grid, a bit like the one shown in Figure 9.1.

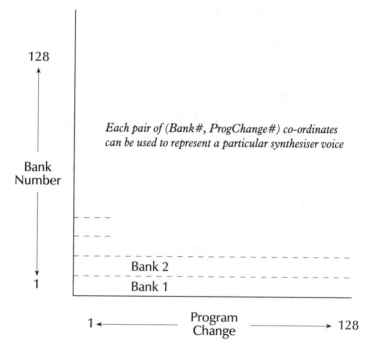

Figure 9.1: The GS approach is based on a two dimensional tone grid.

The GS tone map is rather more complex than Figure 9.1. By defining/reserving the first 64 banks on the 'bank multiplied by program-change' grid the GS standard has allowed for 8192 map defined voices (64 banks of 128 sounds) and they've been arranged in a particularly useful way. Base level preset sounds, called capital tones, reside in program bank 1, with banks 2 to 8 being reserved for variations of those main bank 1 tones.

Bank 1, the capital tones, correspond to the General Midi instrument set and so equipment which conforms to the Roland GS standard also conforms to the General Midi standard. This is why you may hear GS being called a 'superset' of General Midi. Banks 9, 17, 25, 33, 41, 49 and 57 are reserved for use as sub-capital tones, sounds which are related to the captial tone but different enough to be usefully described by some other name.

Intermediate banks offer variations for those tones, so banks 10-16 for instance would contain variations of the bank 9 sounds.

This arrangment has been chosen to allow GS based synths and sound modules to approximate any GS sounds that they do not implement. A module following this arrangement could, if asked to switch to a particular tone variation in a given bank which it did not have, use the sub-capital tone as an approximate equivalent. If that bank wasn't implemented the primary capital root tone could be used so that at least the final voice chosen would be broadly similar to that designated by the original composer of the sequence.

One exception to this 'fallback' scheme concerns the program change area from 121-128. This has been reserved for sound effects. The other exception concerns banks 65-127 which have been designated as an area for user-defined sounds. Bank 128 has been reserved for Roland's MT-32 module factory set sounds.

There are two recently defined additional Midi controller messages that allow for remote bank selection using controllers 0 and 32 (20 hex). The status byte is the standard controller Bn hex and the messages take this form...

Status	*Data-byte-1*	*Data-byte-2*
Bn hex	0 hex	Bank Select MSB (most significant byte)
Bn hex	20 hex	Bank Select LSB (least significant byte)

The GS standard uses only the MSB part, controller 0, to ask a Midi unit to select a particular sound bank. A tonal position on the two-dimensional GS grid can be remotely defined by sending a bank select message and a program change message.

The GS standard also defines drum-note correspondences and again the basic kit (or rather the #35-#81 drum subset of the larger Roland kit) is the same as for General Midi. Provision has been made for alternative drum set support with individual kits selectable by program change commands. Table 9.3 provides the drum note assignment data for the standard set together with an orchestral set and a TR808 drum map for comparison.

Prog # 1 *Standard Set*		*# 26* *TR808 Set*	*# 49* *Orchestra Set*
Note *Name*	*Tone* *Name*	*Tone* *Name*	*Tone* *Name*
D#1 (27)	High Q		Clsd Hi Hat
E1 (28)	Slap		Pedal Hi Hat
F1 (29)	Scratch Push		Open Hi Hat
F#1 (30)	Scratch Pull		Ride Cymbal
G1 (31)	Sticks		
G#1 (32)	Square Click		
A1 (33)	Metronome Click		
A#1 (34)	Metronome Bell		

B1	(35)	Kick Drum 2		Concert B/D 2
C2	(36)	Kick Drum 1	Bass Drum	Concert B/D 1
C#2	(37)	Side Stick	Rim Shot	
D2	(38)	Snare Drum 1	Snare Drum	Concert S/D
D#2	(39)	Hand Clap		Castanets
E2	(40)	Snare Drum 2		Concert S/D
F2	(41)	Low Tom 2	Low Tom 2	Timpani F
F#2	(42)	Closed Hi-Hat	Clsd H/Hat	Timpani F#
G2	(43)	Low Tom 1	Low Tom 1	Timpani G
G#2	(44)	Pedal Hi-Hat	Clsd H/Hat	Timpani G#
A2	(45)	Mid Tom 2	Mid Tom 2	Timpani A
A#2	(46)	Open Hi-Hat	Open H/Hat	Timpani A#
B2	(47)	Mid Tom 1	Mid Tom 1	Timpani B
C3	(48)	High Tom 2	Hi Tom 2	Timpani c
C#3	(49)	Crash Cymbal 1	Cymbal	Timpani c#
D3	(50)	High Tom 1	Hi Tom 1	Timpani d
D#3	(51)	Ride Cymbal 1		Timpani d#
E3	(52)	China Cymbal		Timpani e
F3	(53)	Ride (on Bell)		Timpani f
F#3	(54)	Tambourine		
G3	(55)	Splash Cymbal		
G#3	(56)	Cowbell	Cowbell	
A3	(57)	Crash Cymbal 2		Concert Cymbal 2
A#3	(58)	Vibraslap		
B3	(59)	Ride Cymbal 2		Concert Cymbal 1
C4	(60)	High Bongo		
C#4	(61)	Low Bongo		
D4	(62)	Mute High Conga	High Conga	
D#4	(63)	Open High Conga	Mid Conga	
E4	(64)	Low Conga	Low Conga	
F4	(65)	High Timbale		
F#4	(66)	Low Timbale		
G4	(67)	High Agogo		

G#4	(68)	Low Agogo		
A4	(69)	Cabasa		
A#4	(70)	Maracas	Maracas	
B4	(71)	Short Whistle		
C5	(72)	Long Whistle		
C#5	(73)	Short Quiro		
D5	(74)	Long Guiro		
D#5	(75)	Claves	Claves	
E5	(76)	High Wood Block		
F5	(77)	Low Wood Block		
F#5	(78)	Mute Cuica		
G5	(79)	Open Cuica		
G#5	(80)	Mute Triangle		
A5	(81)	Open Triangle		
A#5	(82)	Shaker		
B5	(83)	Jingle Bell		
C6	(84)	Bell Tree		
C#6	(85)	Castanets		
D6	(86)	Mute Surdo		
D#6	(87)	Open Surdo		
E6	(88)			Applause

Table 9.3: Roland SC55 GS Sound Module - Drum Assignment Information Chart.(Note: Where table entries are blank the drum name is the same as the Standard Percussion Sound).

The GS Standard recommends that channels 10 and 1-6 be regarded as the main channels with the suggested usage being as follows...

Midi Channel	GS Part
10	Rhythm Drums
1	Piano
2	Bass
3	Chord
4	Melody
5	Sub-Chord
6	Sub-Melody

There is quite a bit more to the GS philosophy. The standard lays down a variety of rules concerning the polyphony of each sequence part and provides a number of other specialist controller-based Midi messages that help eliminate the need for including manufacturer-specific sysex data within sequences. It also suggests the use of, and the format for, standardised count-in sequences and so on. Most of this technical information is of interest only to GS developers.

Moving Towards A Goal

The idea behind both GM and GS is to eliminate the need to edit sequence data to get it to sound right on different equipment. The first piece of Roland equipment to support the GS standard was the SC55 sound module, but since then the list has grown to include CM300 and CM500 sound modules, a SCC1 PC sound card, the JV30 synthesizer, the E70, E30 and E15 synthesizers, and many other units. The GM and GS standards are also catching on fast with a great many companies who are in the business of creating ready-made Midi file song arrangements.

This brings me to a point that I should perhaps have mentioned right at the start of my musical wanderings: The General Midi philosophy will only work if the Midi equipment has been built with these ideas in mind. At the moment most potential users of ready made song sequences will not be using GM or GS equipment. This doesn't matter because with a little inside info users can convert sequences very easily. Editing GM or GS sequence data to make it suitable for your Midi set up is no different from editing some other user's data. Throughout this book I've talked about various ways in which sequencer users can make life easier for themselves as far as song creation is concerned.

The ultimate option is of course to buy ready made Midi file arrangements for the songs you'd like to play. The benefits of this approach are reasonably obvious: Firstly, you do not have to be able to physically play the songs in order to use them. Secondly, the arrangements will almost certainly be far better than you could create yourself. Thirdly, you do not have to spend time creating them! For musicians, buying ready made arrangements is the ultimate cheat as far as sequenced music is concerned. For the consumer music market in general, though, this is of no concern and with General Midi now firmly in place this particular market has now started to take off.

One of the reasons that ready made Midi file sequences have not been of that much interest to Midi users in the past is that it was invariably necessary to carry out all manner of 'supplier-specific' editing operations in order to get pre-arranged Midi file material working with particular Midi set ups. Most musicians are not using GM or GS oriented synths and modules at the moment, and this means that some editing of even these standardised sequences will be necessary. The good news is that instead of the previous situation, where you didn't really know what type of editing would be needed until you saw the sequence, with GM and GS based material you will at least have a good idea of what will have to be done. These new General Midi oriented standards have therefore indirectly helped the users of older Midi equipment as well.

10 Tips and Tricks

This chapter contains a lot of unrelated topics that, whilst I thought ought to be mentioned, either didn't properly fit into other discussions or were considered useful enough not to be hidden amongst other material.

Midi and Sequencing

* Running low on memory? Use any memory saver facilities provided by the sequencer. Filter out, or do not generate pitchbend, aftertouch or control change info except for passages where it is particularly important to the song.

* How little do you really need to know to get into Midi sequencing? You must have a general idea of the types of messages that get passed between Midi systems and know roughly how these relate to sequencers and their use. An understanding of how a Midi system must be connected—and the purpose of giving Midi units their own Midi channels—is also needed. After that a little practice with using a sequencer is all that's required, but Midi will invariably seem like a black art to you unless you decide to take an interest in what happens beneath the surface.

* A lot of sequencers allow you to strip out controllers, pitchbend data and aftertouch events and place them on another track. This is useful in two respects. Firstly, it makes editing easier. Secondly, it can help you see just how much data is generated when these facilities are over-used.

* It is often useful to lay down a simple drum track as a guide, along with the basic chords of the composition. This gives you a reasonable harmonic and timing basis for laying down a good bass line track. Once this has been done you can build on this framework, eliminating the early guide tracks as you go.

* When you've created a lot of tracks it is usually a good idea to merge them into a single sequence and then auto-separate them so that data from each Midi channel appears on a different sequencer track. It helps to keep the sequence arrangements tidy.

* Midi Choke. With most of the problems I see involving Midi choke, users don't realise that excessive data transmission is the cause. This seems to be especially so with standalone sequencers because the individual Midi events making up the song are not particularly visible and detailed examination of the events in the sequence is rather impractical.

Often someone comes along and says:'My sequencer seems to be playing up, can you take a look?' I transfer their sequence to a computer based set up and invariably find masses of event data, often containing duplicate events, unnecessarily high density pitchbend data and so on. By removing and thinning I usually find that the sequence, when moved back to the original sequencer, works fine. The point here is that it seems as though users of computer based sequencing equipment are less likely to inadvertently store redundant data because, in general, they are more aware of the data contained in their sequences.

* Pitchbending the same notes on a synth linked to an expander can sometimes result in the units sounding out of tune due to differences in the way each synth interprets the pitchbend information—different tracking rates, bend ranges and so on. Most synths and expanders allow pitchbend recognition to be turned off, and the easiest solution is io do just that—turn off pitchbend recognition in one of the synths.

* When recording a sequence it sounds as though synth voices are playing twice. This is almost certainly what they are doing and it's caused by the sequencer being set up to echo thru its incoming Midi data whilst the synth itself is also generating its own sounds. What happens in this case is that you hit a key, the synth plays the note and the corresponding note-on and note-off Midi messages get sent to the sequencer. Because those messages then get echoed straight back to the synthesizer they trigger the same voice a second time. The solution is to turn off the synthesizer's local on/off control.

* If you have timing problems when trying to transfer Midi sequences by linking two sequencers with a Midi lead, try slowing down the tempo of the source machine. Check that timing problems haven't been caused by something silly like having the quantise settings active on the sequencer that is receiving the data.

* How can you check a Midi lead to see if it's OK or not? Other than the obvious things like checking the DIN plugs for bent or loose connecting pins, and inspecting the cable itself for damage, the best thing to do is to try it. If you suspect that there may be an intermittent fault then try pumping a lot of data through it, a full composition sequencefor example, and whilst doing this encourage the lead to play up by starting from one end and bending or gently pulling the cable whilst listening for glitches, hung notes or anything else untoward. If you are in any doubt after this, replace it.

* Some synths and expanders can build sounds from several voices. It may sound good but it can often reduce the effective polyphony available.

* Notes unexpectedly cut off? It could be voice stealing on a GM/GS synth or module or you may have simply run out of available voices on any synth or expander. Another possible cause could be all notes off messages being generated and recorded in the sequence. Some instruments generate these messages whenever the last held note on a keyboard is released. Check your event lists, the manuals for your equipment, and your sequencer documentation.

* Hung notes whilst sequencing? Did you change Midi channels whilst playing notes with echo thru (soft thru) active? If you did, the appropriate note-off messages probably never got to the synth or expander so the notes you were playing at the time never got cancelled. Your synth may actually have an all notes off panic button that can cancel hung notes, but if not just turn the unit with the offending voices off and on again. Some sequencers allow note-off messages to be lost during editing whilst leaving the corresponding note-on events. This can cause hung notes whilst playing back recorded sequences. Yet another possibility is that you have a faulty or recently disconnected Midi lead in your system.

* Tune Request doesn't seem to work? Units still seem out of tune? Not all synths can act on tune request messages but even with those that do 'tuning' occurs relative to an internal pitch standard and each unit will do its own thing in this respect. Even though the synths may all auto tune to, say, concert A at 440 Hz they may still sound very slightly out of tune with each other after being sent Tune Request messages. This is because the voices in use can themselves make a difference to what does, and what does not, appear to be in tune. For live work, where many of my synth units are used for specific purposes—bass lines, electric piano and so on—I fine tune with the synth's master tuning facilities, using the most commonly used voice on each unit.

* Song Position Pointer (SPP). The basic purpose of these messages is to set all sequence generating units to the same position in a song when they are beginning from a position other than the start of the sequence. Some problems can occur when sequencers take time to relocate themselves after a SPP message arrives but often if the sequencer's SPP function doesn't seem to work it is because the other units involved do not support SPP control. The Midi Implementation Chart shows whether a unit recognises SPP or not.

* Midi Clock messages. If you don't need them, don't send them! Whatever you do, don't use more than one clock source at a time. Few people would do this deliberately but if say a master keyboard or drum machine gets inadvertently set to generate clocks whilst a sequencer is doing the same thing, you can suddenly find your system going crazy for no obvious reason.

Midi Files

* Some sequencers can save sequences in both type 0 and type 1 Midi file formats. Others may not give you a choice or may make a file type decision based on the number of tracks or the type of sequence being written to disk. When you are moving songs between sequencers, the type 1 multi-track Midi file arrangements are to be preferred because tracks are then kept separated and in identical physical order, even though associated channel numbers will, and track names may, vanish.

* Many Midi file players need type 0 files as this is actually the best format for real-time playing since it represents a single stream of Midi events. Sometimes you can encourage a sequencer to write out its data in type 0 format by saving it as a single stream sequence, for example by combining or merging all the track data down to a single track, but if this doesn't work, don't worry, there are plenty of Midi file format converter utilities floating around. Sometimes a sequencer package will provide a separate utility for doing these translations.

* Some sequencers can separate the data held in a type 0 Midi file so that as it is read in the data from each channel gets placed on a separate track. This can be a useful way of splitting up sequence data on sequencers that may not have more obvious channel separation facilities. Take your mixed channel sequence, save it as a type 0 Midi file, read it back into the sequencer and you'll then have the data from each channel on a separate track.

* Some users occasionally experience problems with General Midi or Roland GS instruments and expanders when working with only one expander. General Midi modules have a sort of priority scheme which determines which voices get lost on any occasions where the available polyphony of an instrument is temporarily used up. Priority is always given to the drum channel (10) but after that the order is such that the lower the channel number the higher the GM priority. This means that when recording songs that other people are likely to play you should record the most important of the instrument tracks on the lower numbered channels.

* What can help minimise voice stealing? Firstly, avoid excessive quantising of drums and the instruments of other high priority tracks because these can both encourage voice stealing. What happens is that many notes then get placed on exactly the same time points. It also helps to reduce to the shortest possible the note lengths used for triggering percussion instruments. One last point—don't overuse the sustain pedal because this can also soak up voices like there's no tomorrow.

Percussion Units

* When recording a sequence that is being generated from a drum machine, it sounds as though the drum machine voices are playing twice? This is almost certainly what they are doing, and it's probably caused by the sequencer being set up to echo thru its incoming Midi data. What happens in this case is that you hit a drum pad, the machine plays the note and the corresponding note-on and note-off Midi messages get sent to the sequencer. Because those messages then get immediately echoed back to the drum machine they trigger the same voice a second time.

The solution is to turn off the echo-thru (soft thru) or perhaps disconnect the lead that is returning Midi data to the drum machine. Most drum machines do not have local on/off controls. If by chance yours does, then you could instead set this control to off. That way the first sound that the drum machine automatically generates as a drum pad is pressed would not occur.

* Is it better to use a drum machine as a drum machine or drive it from drum tracks stored in my sequencer, that is use the drum machine just as a percussion voice expander unit? Both methods have advantages. If you keep drum tracks in your sequences then you never have to send Midi clocks, song or pattern select info because you'll just be treating the drummer as a synth expander with a set of preset voices.

You avoid having to program all your drum patterns and arrangements into the drummer and never have to worry about it running short of memory for holding pattern information. It is very convenient to have all instruments tracks, including drums, available for easy sequencer-style editing.

With the alternative approach, using the drum machine as it was to some extent intended to be used, your sequencer doesn't have to hold any drum pattern note material. You just have to add the appropriate song/pattern selection events to your sequences. With this approach you do need to arrange for the sequencer to send Midi clocks in order to keep the sequencer and drum machine in sync. The drum machine in this case needs to be set to its external clock option. Modern drum machines can create all sorts of interesting effects, and some, such as reverse-playing the sound of a sampled drum sound, cannot usually be achieved when driving them via Midi.

The same goes for various rhythm 'swing' effects that are based on extremely small variations in timing. In this respect it is always possible to get more out of a drum machine used in this way. I tend to prefer the former arrangement because it is convenient for editing but it ultimately comes down to personal choice.

* Drum machine goes crazy when you start your sequence, playing far more percussion notes than were programmed into the drum track? You've probably got the drum machine set to its internal clock option. What happens here is that your incoming Midi data causes the drum machine to play its own current pattern as well as playing the notes coming down the Midi line. The solution is to set the drum machine to its Play via Midi mode.

* One way of preparing drum tracks quickly whilst preventing them from sounding mechanical is to record a basic track using standard drum patterns and then subsequently play along with it, recording your efforts as you go. In the final drum track, merge or replace the areas of original drum track with the parts of the manually created tracks that appeal to you.

Miscellaneous

* Keep audio and Midi cables away from cables which are carrying mains power. This is a good general rule whether you are building a home studio or playing live.

* If you've got flight-cased equipment racks then keep as much of the stuff permanently connected inside the case as possible, including a thru box if needed. If you arrange things properly you ought to be able to use just one Midi cable connected to a solitary Midi In for driving everything. This makes setting up both easy and quick.

* If you ever need to you *can* put an ordinary on/off switch or footswitch into a Midi cable—a single pole switch on either of the two non-screen wires. You should only make/break the connection when there is no Midi traffic on the line because you can literally cut a Midi message in half by operating the switch whilst Midi data is flowing. Worse than that, if note off messages get missed you'll end up with hung notes. Most Midi switcher units suffer from exactly the same drawbacks so you should never redirect a Midi stream whilst it is active.

* Don't break earth connections on rack equipment in order to eliminate ground hum. There are ways of reducing earth loop problems by wiring a resistor (3.3k) in line with the screen of the offending item's jack plug. If in doubt check with a friendly audio engineer.

* Very occasionally two pieces of racked equipment can produce what is called 'proximity hum' due to interaction between poorly shielded transformers and other component interactions. The solution is to rearrange the rack layout, physically separating the items causing the problems. If the worst comes to the worst, put one in the top slot of the rack and the other at the bottom.

* Sample Dumping. In recent years there have been some general moves within the music industry towards standardising the transfer of sound sample data. The Midi standard now incorporates an arrangement based on the use of a set of sysex messages that represent something called the Midi Sample Dump standard. The system is quite complicated and includes provision for requesting particular sample types, error checking and communications handshaking. Full technical details can be found in the latest Midi Standard documents.

* With most Midi controlled effects units it's usually possible to create a 'null' program, an effects setting that does nothing. Some units will have settings like these as standard. By setting up the unit so that the null setting can be activated using a program change command you will be able to control the on/off state of the unit automatically. Place a program change command to select the appropriate effect at the start of the song, and then a program change command to select the null program at the end of the song. This is particularly useful for vocal effects because it means that echo, chorus and the like, is then automatically removed from the microphones the moment the song finishes, and you're left with a clean mike for between song announcements, chats and so on. Automating PA/vocal effects like this also means there's less work for the mixing guys to do!

* Learn how to program all of your Midi rack equipment from the front panel, especially how to disable program change voice control, how to select voices and so on. There have been occasions where, due to power fluctuations for example, one or more Midi units have lost their internally memorised data. If a program change table is lost in this way the program change commands embedded in your sequences may no longer select the proper voices for your compositions.

When you're out on a gig it may not be feasible to re-program the program change table on site, but by using the front panel controls to select a suitable voice or voice set and then disabling program change recognition via the front panel controls you may at least be able to get through the night. It is a good idea to make a few notes about these set up procedures and keep them handy, for example taped into the back of the flight-case that holds your Midi units.

Often you'll go years without having a serious problem with a piece of gear, and once you've get say a bass line unit or any other fixed use synth set up for your system you'll hardly ever need to touch it. Believe me, after a year or so you'll have forgotten how to program these units and, since it's not practical to carry the manuals around, a few 'get out of trouble' notes could prove a life saver.

11 Messages and their Meanings

This chapter provides format details for a large number of important types of Midi messages. We start by making the point that at the highest level all Midi messages can be divided into one of two main categories: System messages and Channel messages.

System messages do not contain channel numbers embedded in their status bytes and this is because they will deal with information that is potentially of general interest to all pieces of connected Midi equipment. There are actually three defined subclasses of the system messages group. System Exclusive (sysex) messages, which will not be discussed until chapter 12, System Common messages, and the real-time messages that we're going to look at first.

Real-Time Messages

Real-time (RT) messages contain just a single byte, the status byte, which is actually the whole message. Below are the details of the messages and their values.

Decimal	Hexadecimal	Binary	Title
248	F8	1111 1000	Timing Clock
249	F9	1111 1001	Undefined
250	FA	1111 1010	Start
251	FB	1111 1011	Continue
252	FC	1111 1100	Stop
253	FD	1111 1101	Undefined
254	FE	1111 1110	Active Sensing
255	FF	1111 1111	System Reset

Table 11.1: The Midi Real-Time messages.

Timing clocks are transmitted by sequencers, drum machines, master keyboards and so on as a means of keeping everything in sync. Since they provide a timing reference to be used by all units it's pretty obvious that only one Midi unit should be generating them at any one time. Start, Stop and Continue messages are used to announce the obvious. If, for instance, you hit the start button on a drum machine it will transmit a start message before beginning to transmit the notes which make up its drum pattern. When you cancel the pattern by pressing the stop button, a Midi Stop message will be sent. The System Reset message is a command that can be used to force a piece of equipment to assume a 'just switched on' state.

Active Sensing messages have a much less obvious purpose and are one of a number of background messages that you'll never see in your sequencer event lists. Units which implement active sensing can tell whether there are any communications problems by transmitting dummy data, streams of active sensing messages, during the times when there is no other data on the Midi line.

If a unit which was originally receiving such messages suddenly finds that there is no real Midi data, and no active sensing messages either, then it will switch off its sound generators as a safety precaution. Surprisingly few pieces of Midi equipment actually use active sensing. I have read elsewhere that this is because active sensing bytes impose an additional burden on the often busy Midi communications lines. This simply isn't true. Active sensing messages only ever need to be sent when there is no real Midi data flowing.

System Common Messages

These messages adopt the following layouts...

Decimal	Hexadecimal	Binary	Title
241	F1	1111 0001 0nnn dddd	Midi Time Code Quarter Frame nnn = message type dddd = values
242	F2	1111 0010 0111 1111 0hhh hhhh	Song Position Pointer 1 low data byte high data byte
243	F3	1111 0011 0sss ssss	Song Select song number
244	F4	1111 0100	Undefined
245	F5	1111 0101	Undefined
246	F6	1111 0110	Tune Request
247	F7	1111 0111	End of Sysex message

Table 11.2: The Midi System Common Messages.

Tune Request (decimal 246) asks all synthesizers to tune their oscillators. Song Select (decimal 243 followed by a number from 0 to 127) allows you to specify a song by providing a reference number. If, for instance, you've got a selection of complete songs programmed into a drum machine you can use this message to make selections automatically.

Song Position Pointer messages allow songs and sequences to be started from places other than at the beginning. They're three bytes long and consist of a status byte (decimal 242) followed by the two data bytes which identify the place to start. For the techies the gory details are shown below. The two data bytes are sent as low byte followed by high byte, and because only seven bits of each byte are used you combine the lower seven bits of each data byte to produce a 14-bit number, and it is this number which identifies the starting position. It identifies the Midi beat—one Midi beat equals six clocks—and corresponds to a starting resolution of one semi-quaver in a particular song.

1st byte	2nd byte	3rd byte	Resulting 14-bit number
242	0lll llll	0hhh hhhh	hh hhhh hlll llll
		bit 13	bit 0

A 14-bit number corresponds to the start position in terms of Midi beats.

Channel Messages

Channel messages constitute the largest of the Midi message groups. In the Midi spec itself these messages are divided into two sub-categories: Voice messages, which are concerned with sound production, and Mode messages, which affect the way units interpret the data they handle. The status byte used for mode messages is the same as that used for control change messages. Because of this, mode message descriptions will be dealt with after continuous controllers have been discussed. But first let's look at the voice messages in detail.

Voice Messages

The Midi channel voice messages are concerned with sound production. The seven message types are outlined in table 11.3 below.

Decimal	Hexadecimal	Binary	Title
128+n	8n	1000 nnnn	Note Off
		dddd dddd	note
		vvvv vvvv	velocity
144+n	9n	1111 0010	Note On
		dddd dddd	note
		vvvv vvvv	velocity
160+n	An	1111 0011	Polyphonic key pressure (aftertouch)
		dddd dddd	note
		pppp pppp	pressure value
176+n	Bn	1111 0100	Control change
		dddd dddd	1st data byte
		dddd dddd	2nd data byte
192+n	Cn	1111 0101	Program change
		dddd dddd	patch number
208+n	Dn	1111 0110	Channel pressure (after touch)
		pppp pppp	pressure value
224+n	En	1111 0111	Pitchbend
		dddd dddd	1st data byte
		dddd dddd	2nd data byte

Table 11.3: The Midi Voice Messages.

There's quite a collection, but the ones which get used more than any other are not surprisingly those which turn notes on and off.

When you press a key on a synthesizer keyboard three pieces of data get transmitted. First comes a status byte which announces the fact that a key has been pressed. Second there's a number which identifies the key itself. Middle C is assigned a value of 60 and for every semitone above or below this the note number changes by plus or minus one. Last of all comes a number which tells the receiving equipment how hard this key has been hit. In Midi terms the last piece of information is called the velocity byte and at the end of the day—well, actually in less than 1/1000th of a second—the result is that this sort of information travels down the following Midi lines...

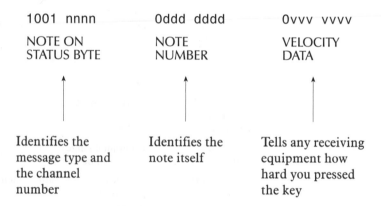

1001 nnnn	0ddd dddd	0vvv vvvv
NOTE ON STATUS BYTE	NOTE NUMBER	VELOCITY DATA

Identifies the message type and the channel number

Identifies the note itself

Tells any receiving equipment how hard you pressed the key

This message format (with one special exception that I'll look at in a moment) is fixed and this means of course that all Midi keyboards have to transmit velocity data, even those without touch sensitivity. The big difference is that touch-sensitive keyboards can work out how hard you've hit the keys, and then translate that pressure into a velocity value between 1 and 127. Non touch-sensitive keyboards just transmit a fixed default value (decimal 64) instead.

Note-Off Messages

As you release keys on the keyboard that were being held down, streams of messages must be transmitted to indicate the notes that are to be turned off. The Midi standard allows two ways of doing this. Firstly the keyboard can send an equivalent note-off message. This also contains three bytes but although it takes exactly the same form as a note-on message, it uses a different status byte...

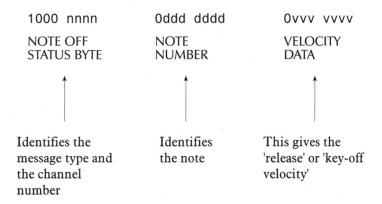

A second way that note-off information can be transmitted is by sending note-on messages using zero for the velocity value. With this approach the equipment loses the ability to transmit a release velocity value, but it gains an important potential advantage in another area.

When the second approach is used the messages which turn notes on and off are transmitted solely in terms of streams of Midi's note-on messages. Why is that useful? It just so happens that part of the Midi specification defines something called 'running status', which allows all messages after the first one to be transmitted without their status bytes - providing they form part of a stream of identical message types. So the benefit of turning notes on and off using note-on messages is that running status allows a third of the transmitted data to be eliminated, and that can be quite a significant saving.

Program Change

The program change message defined by the Midi standard is a two-byte message which takes the following form.

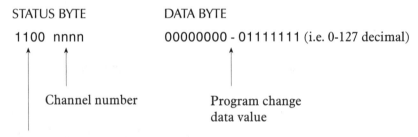

STATUS BYTE

1100 nnnn

Channel number

This part of the status byte indicates that the message is a program change

DATA BYTE

00000000 - 01111111 (i.e. 0-127 decimal)

Program change
data value

The status byte identifies the message type and a Midi channel. The trailing data byte gives a value from 0 to 127 decimal which indicates a program change value. In effect then these messages allow the selection of any one of 128 different possible 'programs'. For instance the two bytes C0 hex (decimal 192) followed by 0 hex (decimal 0) tells any unit set to Midi channel 1 to change to its program 0 voice arrangement setting. As mentioned earlier you'll find that some sequencers and synths will expect the range 1-128 to be used, others will work with 0-127, the range actually stored in the messages.

Because of this you may need to adjust values by +1 or - 1 to get the right effects with certain equipment. Let's suppose that your sequencer uses 0-127 for its program change events and you want to add a command to the start of a sequence track so that the synth memory patch #5 is selected. Well, if the synth used a 1-128 style patch command range then you'd need to insert a program change #4 command into the sequence instead. Confused? Think about it!

Polyphonic Aftertouch (Polyphonic Key Pressure)

Some Midi keyboards respond not only to the initial velocity with which keys have been hit but to variations in pressure after the keys have been held down. These pressure variations are translated into individual key-pressure messages and transmitted whenever a change of pressure is detected.

Sounds great? Yes it is, but keyboards which offer true polyphonic aftertouch are also very expensive. Most keyboards opt for the more economic 'average pressure' approach, sending overall channel pressure messages instead (see below). One of the disadvantages of true polyphonic aftertouch is the amount of extra Midi data which gets transmitted.

This causes two problems: Firstly, the extra data can contribute to the so-called Midi clogging problems, where so much data goes down the Midi lines that things from a communications viewpoint start to go wrong. Secondly, you'll be eating up a lot more sequencer memory because of the extra data it has to store. Polyphonic aftertouch messages are three bytes long and, in terms of the binary numbers transmitted, have the following type of format.

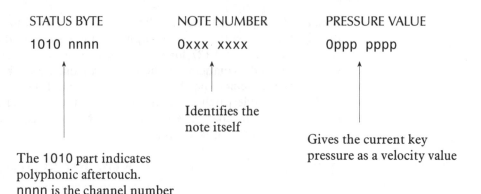

STATUS BYTE

1010 nnnn

The 1010 part indicates
polyphonic aftertouch.
nnnn is the channel number

NOTE NUMBER

0xxx xxxx

Identifies the
note itself

PRESSURE VALUE

0ppp pppp

Gives the current key
pressure as a velocity value

Channel Aftertouch (Channel Key Pressure)

These provide a sort of average pressure which applies to all notes sounding. Keyboards which transmit this type of data send aftertouch messages which contain two bytes. The message format looks like this...

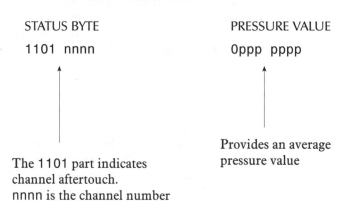

STATUS BYTE

1101 nnnn

The 1101 part indicates
channel aftertouch.
nnnn is the channel number

PRESSURE VALUE

0ppp pppp

Provides an average
pressure value

Pitchbend (Pitchwheel) Messages

These messages are sent whenever the pitch wheel or lever changes position, and they take the form shown below.

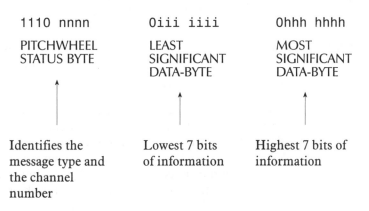

1110 nnnn	0iii iiii	0hhh hhhh
PITCHWHEEL STATUS BYTE	LEAST SIGNIFICANT DATA-BYTE	MOST SIGNIFICANT DATA-BYTE
Identifies the message type and the channel number	Lowest 7 bits of information	Highest 7 bits of information

Midi's Controller Messages

Midi has some messages specifically allocated to a set of 'controllers'. By sending a synthesizer the right type of controller messages it's possible to modify certain synthesizer effects just as if you were fiddling with the synthesizer controls themselves. Similarly, when real synthesizer controls such as the mod-wheel are touched, the synthesizer itself will generate an appropriate controller message.

The Midi standard defines continuous controllers, meant to simulate rotary controls, and on/off switch type controllers, but in terms of the structure of the Midi messages they all have the following three byte arrangement.

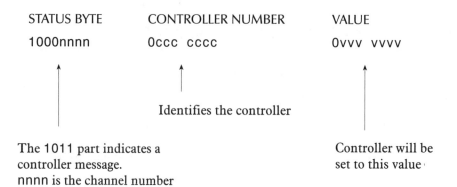

STATUS BYTE   CONTROLLER NUMBER   VALUE

1000nnnn   0ccc cccc   0vvv vvvv

Identifies the controller

The 1011 part indicates a
controller message.
nnnn is the channel number

Controller will be
set to this value

Some controllers have Midi standard recommeded uses. A synthesizer's mod-wheel for instance should generate controller #1 messages, Midi volume messages should use controller #7. Your synth manual will tell you what controllers, if any, your synthesizer transmits or understands. The important thing to realize is that these message-to-effect relationships are 'soft' and at the end of the day it is the synth manufacturer who decides how a particular synth will respond to particular controller messages.

In some cases the message-to-effect relationships can be changed by altering the internal settings of the synthesizer itself, and these synthesizers are said to have 'assignable controllers'. Such a synth could, when receiving mod-wheel messages, be made to use those values to alter a completely different effect. Similarly, it might be able to modify its mod-wheel settings when receiving messages on a controller other than the conventional mod-wheel controller #1.

These type of controller assignment facilities, which are manufacturer dependent, are very useful but are normally only found on the more expensive synthesizers.

Midi's controller messages are an area that seem to cause more confusion than might be expected. Part of this stems from the fact that a lot of people seem to be under the impression that there are many different types of controller messages involving switches, continuous controllers, and both high and low resolution facilities.

It is certainly true that several different types of Midi controller are available, but as already explained there is only one type of Midi controller message. It's the various categories of controller use that seem to fox people, so here are some detailed notes. The first byte, the status byte, is the value B0 hex combined with a channel number. The two bytes which follow the status byte are both Midi data bytes, so they can only take values between 0 and 127 (0 hex and 7F hex).

The second byte of a controller message is termed a controller number and although it could take values as high as 127 it's actually limited to 120 for controller number purposes. The Midi specification has used values 121-127 for other purposes that we're going to look at shortly.

Another simplification is that, at the moment, the controller numbers 102-120 are undefined, so you don't really need to worry about them. We can also, as far as general discussions go, knock out the 96-101 controller range because these have been assigned for rather specialized uses.

That, to all intents and purposes, brings us down to a set of controller numbers from 0 to 95 and these are split into two groups, switch controls and continuous controls, which I'll now explain in detail.

Switch Controllers

The switch controllers (there are 32 of them) are the easiest to deal with because they're just the Midi equivalent of an on/off switch. The third byte of a switch message can take one of two values—0, which means that the switch is off, and 127 (7F hex) which means that the switch is on. Switch messages therefore look like this...

Status byte	*controller number*	*controller value*
Bn (hex)	(between 64 and 95)	(0 or 127)
byte 1	byte 2	byte 3

For controller switch use, the controller data values which fall between 0 and 127 (values 1-126) are meaningless and are ignored. This definition is a bit wasteful of byte-space but a more efficient bit encoding scheme, perhaps representing seven switches per single controller message (using one bit per switch), would have meant that such messages would take longer for the receiving equipment to decode.

Examples? If you look at the Midi Implementation sheet for Yamaha's TX81Z expander you'll see that switch numbers 64 and 65 are used to control sustain and portamento. Since 65 decimal = 41 hex it's not too difficult to work out that if the unit was set to channel 16 the message which would turn the portamento on would consist of the three values BF hex, 41 hex, and 7F hex. The equivalent message which turns the portamento off would just use a zero last byte rather than the 7F hex 'switch on' value.

Continuous Controllers

Controller numbers 0-63 are known as continuous controllers and these are probably the worst offenders as far as confusion goes. To start with they do *not* represent 64 different controllers, they're only meant to represent 32 physical devices. Here's the reason why.

A continuous controller can be thought of as an analogue dial which can be adjusted from a low value, zero, to a high value which has the numerical value 3FFF hex. If you convert these to decimal values you'll find that means these controllers can be adjusted from 0 to 16383. These number ranges were selected so that a reasonably high resolution—a 'dial' containing many different intermediate states—could be used.

From the viewpoint of those who defined the Midi standard the use of continuous controllers presented two problems: First of all the proposed high resolution might not always be needed. Second, because a single controller message can only carry a 7-bit controller value, some alternative means of representing the full controller value (which needs 14 bits) had to be found.

The solution, which has been subjected to more than its fair share of criticism, was as follows: If you look at the 3FFF hex maximum value and express it in binary form you'll see that it does indeed need 14 bits since 3FFF hex = 11 1111 1111 1111 binary. Now, if you take those bits and divide them into two groups, you end up with two groups each consisting of seven bits. The left-hand group contains the most significant bits of the number, the right-hand group the least significant bits.

If you look back at the generalized controller message you'll see that there's only space for *one* data value. So how are continuous controller messages sent which need the full 14 bits, need two data bytes that is, to specify the controller position? It's easy. *Two* different controller messages are transmitted. How do you tell which part of the data value is being transmitted? Each continuous controller is assigned *two* different controller numbers.

One controller number says 'here comes a new value for the highest seven bits of the controller data value', the other says 'here comes a new value for the lower seven bits'. Which values are used? Controllers 0-31 carry the most significant bits (MSB), Controllers 32-63 carry the least significant bits (LSB). Controllers 0-31 and controllers 32-63 are therefore paired and in reality each pair (0/32, 1/33, 2/34) would represent the values destined for the same physical controller.

The Midi standard, in an attempt to save space on the communications lines, allows for partial transmission of these continuous controller data values. It states that it is only necessary to send both parts of the controller value if both parts are needed and both parts have changed in value. In other words if a manufacturer only wants to implement some particular low resolution controller facility they can arrange to transmit and recognize controller messages using a controller number between 0 and 31.

By taking the Yamaha TX81Z mod-wheel control as an example I'll be able to show how this works in practice: In general, Midi Controller 1 is designated as the modulation wheel's MSB and controller 33 represents the LSB part. Yamaha's TX81Z implementation chart shows that the unit recognizes controller number 1 messages, but doesn't recognize controller 33 messages. In other words it shows that Yamaha have implemented low resolution mod-wheel control.

Nothing can change this, so even if a keyboard could send high resolution mod-wheel messages to the TX81Z (which would actually consist of a combination of controller 1 and controller 33 messages) the TX81Z, because it only understands the controller 1 messages, would still provide low resolution response.

In general, the use of high resolution controllers means that more data has to be transmitted but, as I mentioned earlier, it's not always necessary for the sending equipment to transmit both parts of the controller's data values. If some recognized physical control movement results only in a change in the LSB part of the controller value, then only one controller message (the LSB part) need be sent.

The controllers specified in the Midi standard are then basically a description, a logical blue-print, of 32 switches and 32 'dial type' continuous controllers. The relationship between the controllers and particular effects is 'soft', that is it exists only in the eyes of the software which controls the transmitting and receiving equipment.

A lot of controllers now have standard recommended uses (1=mod-wheel, 2=breath-control, 7=volume) but it's unlikely that we'll ever see 100% standardization, so synths and expanders with assignable controllers will always give you just that bit more flexibility as far as long term Midi controller use goes.

Mode Messages

I mentioned that the controller messages whose first data byte values lie between 121 and 127 are reserved for a special use. These messages, which are known as Mode messages, consist of the following group.

Decimal	Hexadecimal	Binary	Title
176+n	Bn	1000 nnnn cccc cccc vvvv vvvv	Control Change = 121 Reset All Controllers = 0
176+n	Bn	1000 nnnn cccc cccc vvvv vvvv	Control Change = 122 Local Control = 0 Local Control Off or 1 Local Control On
176+n	Bn	1000 nnnn cccc cccc vvvv vvvv	Control Change = 123 All Notes Off = 0
176+n	Bn	1000 nnnn cccc cccc vvvv vvvv	Control Change = 124 Omni Mode Off = 0
176+n	Bn	1000 nnnn cccc cccc vvvv vvvv	Control Change = 125 Omni Mode On = 0
176+n	Bn	1000 nnnn cccc cccc vvvv vvvv	Control Change = 126 Mono Mode On = number of channels
176+n	Bn	1000 nnnn cccc cccc vvvv vvvv	Control Change = 127 Poly Mode On = 0

Table 11.4: The Midi mode mmessages group.

The first three message in this group have fairly obvious uses. Reset all controllers does exactly that - it causes a Midi unit to reset its controllers to what is chosen (by the manufacturer) to be an ideal initial state. The local control on/ off message, which we first mentioned in chapter 2, allows the keyboard/sound-circuitry of a synth to be severed or reinstated. The all notes off command basically does exactly what you'd expect, although not all Midi instruments recognise this command and the Midi standard itself provides some quite complicated guidelines concerning the situations where it can safely be used.

Of more interest at the moment are what might be called the 'real' Midi mode messages. Synthesizers contain sound generators, voices, and 'voice assignment' is the term given to the process of routing note-on and note-off data from the keyboard (or Midi terminals) to the voice circuitry—so that the right notes are played with the right sounds. With Midi the relationship between the 16 available channels and the voices also has to be defined and here the Midi standard specifies separate modes of operation. These modes can usually be selected either by front panel operations or remotely via an appropriate Midi message.

There are two variables involved: The first option is whether the unit is going to receive data on *all* 16 channels or not—the term for the former state is Omni On, for the latter it is Omni Off. In short, when you select a mode that is Omni On based, every channel message that the unit receives will be acted upon and this means that you lose the benefits of channel selectivity! The other characteristic that is under your control is whether you specify polyphonic or monophonic operation. Here the situation tends to get a bit complicated. Mono, when on, restricts the assignments of voices to just one voice per channel. With Poly On (Poly On = Mono Off), any number of voices can be assigned by the Midi unit's voice assignment mechanism.

The various pairs of combinations of these choices leads to four possibilities and the Midi standard sets out the definitions shown in tables 11.5 and 11.6.

MODE	OMNI	POLY	
1	ON	ON	Voice messages are received on *all* channels and assigned to voices polyphonically
2	ON	OFF	Voice messages are received on *all* (ie Mono On) channels but control only one voice.
3	OFF	ON	Voice messages are received on the selected channel N and are assigned to voices polyphonically.
4	OFF	OFF	Voice messages are received in (ie Mono On) voices N, up to (N + M - 1) and are assigned monophonically to voices 1 thru M. The number of voices is specified by the third byte of the Mono Mode message.

Table 11.5: Receiving equipment mode definitions for a receiver assigned to a basic channel N.

MODE	OMNI	POLY	
1	ON	ON	Voice messages are transmitted on channel N
2	ON	OFF	One voice message is sent on (ie MonoOn) channel N
3	OFF	ON	Voice messages are transmitted on selected channel N
4	OFF	OFF	Voice messages for voices 1 thru M (Mono On) are transmitted in voice channels N thru (N + M - 1).

Table 11.6: Transmitting equipment mode definitions for transmitters assigned to channel N.

Well, that covers the details. Now for the question which everyone asks at one time or other... What does it all mean?

Here's a condensed version of the main ideas: Mode 1, because it disregards channel info, is really only useful as a 'failsafe' mode. A unit set to Mode 1 will respond to any and every channel message it receives. It's useful for troubleshooting, checking leads and so on, but there are very few occasions where you would deliberately want a single unit to respond to data from all channels!

Mode 2 (Omni On / Mono) is another mode which ignores channel selectivity. You can forget about this mode altogether— rumour has it that the definition was a mistake and it certainly has no obvious advantages or uses.

Mode 3 (Omni Off / Poly On) is the most widely used of all the Midi modes. Synthesizers will transmit polyphonic data on the selected channel, and any receiving equipment which is in this mode and set to receive on the same channel will interpret and use the information to play polyphonically.

Mode 4 is rather special. With Mode 4 selected each synthesizer voice gets its own channel number. With an eight note polyphonic synthesizer tuned to basic channel 1 the first voice responds to data received on channel 1, the second to data on channel 2 and so on. In other words, Mode 4 uses a user-definable set of Midi channels for its operations. As far as specific applications go, Midi guitar control for example, there are some grey areas related to the use of Mode 4 but there's no doubt that it does have some interesting potential applications.

Although there are only four official Midi modes, the facilities now offered on some expander units have added an interesting new slant to the Midi mode debate. Many multi-timbral expanders and synthesizers can now be set up to behave as though they are two or more completely separate synthesizers, each controlling their own voices and responding to their own channels. Some of Mode 4's uses have therefore been rather quenched by the multi-timbral facilities now available with many units.

Explaining the Midi Mode messages is easy. They are three bytes long and all have the same status byte. You'll see it written in binary as 1011nnnn where the lower four bits 'nnnn' are the binary form of the channel number. The data bytes which follow allow you to set Omni Mode On (decimal 125, 0), Omni Mode Off (decimal 124, 0), Mono Mode On (decimal 126 followed by a byte specifying the number of channels) and Poly Mode On (decimal 127, 0).

Midi Clogging

Polyphonic key pressure messages, controller messages and pitchbend messages can (in certain circumstances) be sent down the Midi lines in vast quantities. Because of this, their indiscriminate use can lead to two types of problems. Firstly, sequencer memory can get eaten up like there's no tommorow and this is one of the reasons why most sequencers allow these types of messages to be selectively filtered out if they are not required.

Secondly, you may experience problems owing to the fact that too much information is being transmitted. This latter effect can result in intermittent faults involving lost or stuck notes and is commonly known as a 'Midi clogging' or 'Midi choke' effect.

Status Byte Structure

I have been asked on many occasions why the Midi Standard doesn't get altered so that it can include more channels. It dawned on me that although a lot has been written about Midi messages, their layouts and their uses, no one seems to have dealt with the structure of these messages from an overall plan type of viewpoint. Since it is the Midi spec's status byte structure definition that limits the variety of Midi messages that can be formed, it seems worthwhile spending some time discussing how the various message classes are created.

But before this let's remind ourselves about the main categories of messages that Midi supports. At the highest level it distinguishes between channel messages (those which contain a channel number) and system messages. Channel messages can be one of two types: voice messages, which are concerned with creating melodies and rhythms and selecting various sounds, and mode messages which define a number of different message interpretation schemes. System messages deal with the transmission of information of general interest to the Midi system and they come in three forms known as common, real-time and system exclusive (sysex).

For the following discussions it is only the status byte layout that concerns us. Status byte values, as you'll now know, always have the most significant bit of the byte (bit 7) set high. This distinction is only the beginning of the hierarchy that exists within the multi-byte Midi message system, but already it's not hard to see that this scheme immediately limits the number of different messages that Midi can use because there are effectively only seven bits of the status byte available to represent different message types.

Now let's look at the status byte bits b6-b4. These bits can form eight different patterns: 000, 001, 010, 011, 100, 101, 110 and 111. Seven of these bit patterns are used to define channel messages like this...

b6	*b5*	*b4*	*Message type*
0	0	0	Note Off
0	0	1	Note On
0	1	0	Polyphonic Key Pressure
0	1	1	Control Change
1	0	0	Program Change
1	0	1	Channel Pressure
1	1	0	Pitch Bend Change

These bit patterns have been designated as channel messages. Where does the channel number go? It's stored in the lowest four bits (b3-b0)of the status byte number. Channel numbers 1-16 are stored internally as the numbers 0-15, so a note-off status byte for channel 1 is represented like this...

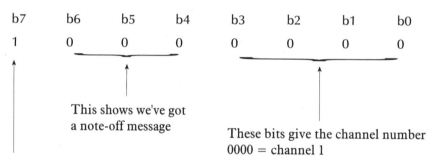

b7	b6	b5	b4	b3	b2	b1	b0
1	0	0	0	0	0	0	0

This shows we've got
a note-off message

These bits give the channel number
0000 = channel 1

This is the status byte
indicator bit

This, incidentally, explains why the 16 conventional Midi channels limit exists: Four bits (b3-b0) can store *only* 16 different patterns: 0000, 0001, 0010, 0011, 0100, 0101, 0110, 0111, 1000, 1001, 1010, 1011, 1100, 1101, 1110, and 1111. So, unless the whole of the status byte was completely redefined and expanded, it's just not possible to include more than 16 separate channels.

In defining the channel message status bytes the bit patterns have taken up all of the combinations in the upper four bits, except for one—the pattern 1111. I didn't include this bit combination in the above discussion because it has nothing to do with channel messages at all. It has been reserved for various system messages...

b6	b5	b4	*Message type*
1	1	1	System messages

For these system messages, bits b6-b4 can only take the value 111 because all of the other combinations have been used to represent channel message types. So how are the system messages represented? It's easy. Remember, system messages do not have a channel number, so bits b3-b0 can be used to identify 16 different types of system message. What happens is that b3 is used to indicate one of two different message subclasses. If the value of b3 is zero then we have the group that, with the exception of the sysex status byte—which defines its own special group of 'non-standard' messages—are collectively called the System Common messages. Here are the bit values so you can see how they fit into the overall scheme of things...

b3	b2	b1	b0	*Message Type*
0	0	0	0	Sysex Message
0	0	0	1	Midi Time Code
0	0	1	0	Song Position Pointer
0	0	1	1	Song Select
0	1	0	0	Undefined
0	1	0	1	Undefined
0	1	1	0	Tune Request
0	1	1	1	End of System Exclusive

If bit 3 is set high (to 1) we get the other sub-group, the real-time message group...

b3	b2	b1	b0	Message Type
1	0	0	0	Timing Clock
1	0	0	1	Undefined
1	0	1	0	Start
1	0	1	1	Continue
1	1	0	0	Stop
1	1	0	1	Undefined
1	1	1	0	Active Sensing
1	1	1	1	System Reset

Well, that's covered the ideas behind the status byte reasonably thoroughly. On the face of it knowing about these bit patterns may seem to be only of academic interest. It could however have one important use to you if, that is, you become interested in writing computer programs which read and interpret Midi messages. At this stage an understanding of these status byte layouts becomes essential. There is a lot of Midi programming that can be quite easily done using high-level languages like Basic, and since there are an awful lot of Basic programmers around nowadays this is a topic that I make a point of returning to later in the book.

12 Sysex Messages

Despite the acceptance of the basic message framework of the Midi standard it was recognised right from the start that most equipment manufacturers would also need a way of providing their own, specialised control data. The Midi standard steering committee came up with an excellent solution—a data packet, called a system exclusive or sysex message that could be easily recognised but which could contain absolutely anything a manufacturer might require.

The basic idea is simple. With a sysex message it is only the outside of the information packet, the shell as it were, that is fixed. The layout of the internal information, the real data, is left to the organisation who creates the message. As far as the outer shell of the sysex message is concerned the format looks like this...

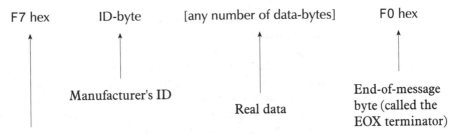

Any manufacturer who wants to implement specialist functions, functions which the basic Midi messages were not designed to handle, can therefore do it very easily. In recent years there has been an increasing trend towards implementing all sorts of voice modification and control functions, and in fact many pieces of equipment now offer almost full sysex message remote-control.

One of the potential dangers of sending non-standard messages around a Midi system would be the likelihood of misinterpretation. If a specialised sysex message meant for a Roland unit started to be interpreted by a Casio device it would be unlikely to make any sense of it. Worse than that a misinterpreted message could cause damage, perhaps scrambling important memory locations and destroying voice settings into the bargain. The second byte in a sysex message, the manufacturer ID code, serves to protect against that type of occurrence. If a unit doesn't recognise the ID code then it ignores the message altogether.

Control of synthesizer voice uploading and downloading was an obvious use of sysex messages. In chapter 2 you may remember I mentioned that synthesizer voice programming could be a time consuming affair. I was talking primarily about voice programming using the synthesizer's front-panel controls, but nowadays this is not the only approach. It is also possible to edit the voices of many synthesizers using computer programs that provide easy-to-use graphical interfaces. These programs, known as patch or voice editors, are now becoming very sophisticated and almost all provide editing and general voice-library load/save facilities.

How do they work? It's all done with sysex messages. When you ask a patch editor program to upload a voice from a synthesizer it will send the synthesizer a dump request sysex message. If all goes well the synthesizer will respond by sending back the data using another sysex message, one designed to hold bulk voice data. Similarly, you may touch a slider on the patch editor's screen and hear a change in the voice being edited. What has happened is that the patch editor detected the slider change, transmitted another sysex message, and that message (when received by the synth) produced the voice change. It is then sysex messages that allow patch editors to perform their magic. The possibilities for other types of equipment control are endless!

Manufacturers are expected to provide details of the formats of their system exclusive messages. Most do, and it is usually very well presented. In recent years, incidentally, a number of universal control sysex messages have been added to the Midi standard, and there is even a special sysex message ID (7D hex) which is reserved for non-commercial applications—for schools, research and so on.

Using Sysex Control

Many synths, expanders and other Midi units nowadays have a set of more esoteric control facilities that can usually only be accessed via sysex messages. Most users do not need to either worry about or use sysex control but a general appreciation of what can be done is quite useful. Let's get a couple of things straight: There's usually nothing complex about the inner contents of a sysex message, so if I or anyone else knows about the inner contents of particular messages it's not because we're gifted with magical powers of deductive reasoning, it's just because we knew where to look up the necessary details! Those details are obtained either from equipment manuals or by pestering manufacturers until they come up with the goods.

The trouble with all this stuff however is that it is Midi unit specific. So if you want examples of what sysex control can do for you the place to look is your own equipment manuals. Be warned though - the descriptions can seem complicated at first, because they invariably use hexadecimal numbers or bit-oriented descriptions when describing the layout of the data. If you are not into this type of number manipulation then experimenting with sysex control is an area best left alone.

For those who are not put off by alien number forms it may be useful to look at a couple of sysex-oriented examples.

One difficulty with sysex control is that a manufacturer will often need to transmit numbers larger than 127. At other times they may need to transmit numbers which could be expressed using only a few 'bits' of a data-byte. In this latter case, using a whole data-byte to transmit information—like an on/off state which can be represented by a single 'bit'—wastes valuable communications space. So manufacturers sometimes spread numerical data across several Midi data-bytes, and at other times will represent multiple items within one single data-byte. It's rather unfortunate, but the simple truth of the matter is that recognising and 'unpacking' these somewhat strange number formats can only be done if you're happy playing around with binary and hexadecimal numbers.

Here's a specific example of a TX81Z sysex bulk dump message layout. One of the sysex messages which the TX81Z understands is known as the Program Change Table Bulk Data Format. The TX81Z has a user definable program change table which allows you to define exactly which voices are selected by particular program change commands. Sound-wise there are four banks—A, B, C, and D—each containing 32 preset voices, an I bank containing a further 32 user programmable voices, and a performance-mode bank of 24 combination settings. That's 128 + 32 + 24 = 184 possible alternatives, and you can select any of these using a program change command. But there are only 128 different program change numbers, so how can you access 184 settings? In actual fact you can't, and what the TX81Z's Program Change Table does is let you choose which 128 of the 184 settings the commands will access.

To represent 184 different selections needs an 8-bit binary number. Normally this could be represented using one 8-bit byte but because a single Midi data-byte can only represent a 7-bit number, because the highest bit of a data-byte must be set low, Yamaha have to use two Midi data-bytes to represent any given table entry. In short, the contents of the Program Change Table has to be transmitted and received using a sysex message which includes data laid out as below.

Layout of the data-byte   Effective data contents

b7   b6   b5   b4   b3   b2   b1   b0

←————— set to zero —————→   msb   0 - 1

0   ← remainder of binary number →   0 - 127
        (i.e. number *without* the msb)

When the TX81Z transmits a Program Change Table dump it sends 128 such entries as part of a sysex message. The convention used to represent particular voices within such a table has been defined by Yamaha to be as follows...

Bank I	voices numbered from 0-31
Bank A	voices numbered from 32-63
Bank B	voices numbered from 64-95
Bank C	voices numbered from 96-127
Bank D	voices numbered from 128-159
Performance Memories	PF settings numbered from 160-183

One way of increasing the flexibility of the TX81Z's Program Change Table facilities would be to create sequences which contained these sorts of tables and have the appropriate table sent to the expander prior to starting the song.

Few people find it necessary to get involved with this type of control, although sometimes you might have to write short Sysex messages to encourage pieces of Midi equipment to dump their data to a patch librarian. Supposing for example that we needed to write a sysex message that caused the TX81Z to transmit its voice data. By looking in the TX81Z's manual we find seven such messages listed and these include single or multiple Voice Dumps (VCEM and VMEM), one or all Performance Memories (PCED and PMEM) and system and microtune details. Yamaha give the message layouts using 'n' for the TX81Z's basic receive channel, like this...

VCED	F0, 43, 2n, 03, F7
VMEM	F0, 43, 2n, 04, F7
ACED + VCED	F0, 43, 2n, 7E, "LM__8976AE", F7
PCED	F0, 43, 2n, 7E, "LM__8976PE", F7
PMEM	F0, 43, 2n, 7E, "LM__8976PM", F7
System Setup	F0, 43, 2n, 7E, "LM__8976Sx", F7 (x = 0, 1, 2)
Micro Tune	F0, 43, 2n, 7E, "LM__MCRTEx", F7 (x = 0, 1)

Suppose we want to ask the TX81Z to send its VMEM data? We've got the overall message layout and are just left with the job of including the right basic receive channel value. Yes, you've guessed it, it's down to a bit of binary/hex conversion again. Suppose your TX81Z is set to channel 15. Have we got to make n=15? No, Midi channels are named as channels 1-16 but internally all units use the equivalent of 0-15 decimal. So if we're set to channel 15 then the channel number used in the request-message needs to be the hex equivalent of decimal 14— E hex, that is.

In other words the VMEM request...	F0	43	2n	04	F7
becomes...	F0	43	2E	04	F7

So that's it. If we place the five hex numbers F0, 43, 2E, 04 and F7 into our librarian program's dump request initialisation string then that message, when transmitted to the Yamaha TX81Z, will cause it to respond (providing it is set to channel 15) by sending back its **VMEM** voice data to the librarian program.

There are many other sysex possibilities. With the TX81Z it is for instance possible to control various front panel switches by remote control. Two of these switches control the master volume, the overall volume setting applied to all channels and voices of this multi-timbral unit. The manual shows the overall internal form of the associated sysex message like this...

F0 hex	Sysex status byte
43 hex	Yamaha ID
1n hex	Basic receive channel
0gggggghh	group number and sub-group number
0ppppppp	parameter number
0ddddddd	data
F7 hex	End of sysex message

The manual also tells us a few other things. Switch parameter 73 decreases the master volume setting by 1, and switch parameter 74 increases the master volume by 1. For remote control setting the group number is decimal 4, the sub-group number is decimal 3 and for the master volume control the decimal numbers 73 and 74 increase or decrease the current setting by a factor of 1 respectively.

What does the entry called 'data' mean? The manual says 0 = switch-off and 127 = switch-on, but from the table layout it looks as though that particular byte only applies to the power-on/reset remote control switch. When I first read the manual I wasn't absolutely sure what value should be used for that 'data' entry, although in hindsight it was obvious. But I knew that I'd be able to find out by doing a few experiments and that's what this particular example is all about.

Firstly I picked one of the messages (the volume decrease) and filled in the info gleaned from the manual. For convenience the hex and binary numbers were converted to decimal values at this stage. Notice, incidentally, how Yamaha have squashed the group/sub-group values into a single Midi data-byte to save space. For our example the group/sub-group value is 0 00100 11 hex—19 decimal. After playing around with a few numbers I decided that the full decrease master volume sysex message would take the following form...

240 decimal	Sysex status byte
67 decimal	Yamaha ID
30 decimal	16+ Bbsic receive channel(-1) of my own TX81Z unit
19 decimal	group number and (hh) sub-group number
73 decimal	parameter number for volume *decrease*
0 ?	some data value ? - not really sure
247 decimal	End of sysex message

A seven byte sysex message—240, 67, 30, 19, 73, 0, ?, 247—with one questionable data value. To check that I'd read the manual properly I built these values into a short sequence and sent it to my TX81Z unit. In this case I used Dr T's KCS sequencer which allows lists of single byte Midi events to be created easily. The first event-list trial looked like this...

Measure	*Event*	*Type*
1-1	1	*240
1-1	2	*67
1-1	3	*30
1-1	4	*19
1-1	5	*73
1-1	6	*0
1-1	7	*247

I plugged in the TX81Z, sent the sysex message and... nothing happened. The next thing to try was changing that dubious zero value in event number 6. The manual had mentioned the value 127, so I tried that. The result? Success. The display changed to Master Volume showing the current volume value, and each time a message was set the volume setting decreased by one. The only trouble was the TX81Z parameter screen stuck on the Master Volume display and didn't revert to the normal voice setting display after the message had been received.

I then realised what was happening. Sending this particular message is equivalent to pushing the buttons on the control panel which (on the TX81Z) produce the Master Volume display setting. Perhaps an equivalent message with event 6 = zero would effectively release those buttons and bring the display back to normal? Yes it did, although it also resulted in a second decrease in the value of the Master Volume setting.

At least by now the purpose of that questionable data byte had been determined. So if I'd wanted to decrease the Master Volume setting of the TX81Z by 5, I could do it by sending these five short sysex messages...

Measure	Event	Type	
1-1	1	*240	
1-1	2	*67	
1-1	3	*30	Four of these sysex
1-1	4	*19	messages would cause the
1-1	5	*73	Master Volume setting to
1-1	6	*127	decrease by 4
1-1	7	*247	

Measure	Event	Type	
1-1	1	*240	
1-1	2	*67	
1-1	3	*30	This last message brought the
1-1	4	*19	display back to it's original
1-1	5	*73	form and gave the final
1-1	6	*0	Master Volume decrease
1-1	7	*247	

By replacing the value switch 73 with a value of 74 the same messages would provided equivalent sysex controlled Master Volume setting increases.

Last Words

That gives you a glimpse of what sysex control is all about. Apologies for the fact that this example had to be equipment specific but there was no other way to give detailed examples of how things are controlled with sysex messages. You'll probably find notes about your own equipment's sysex facilities in your user manuals. All your synths and expanders will have different ways of doing things but most manufacturers do provide enough useful information to get you started on the right track.

The rest? Working out what bytes need to be sent comes down to your interpretation of the info present in the manuals, and this involves common sense, lots of practice in binary/hex conversion and sometimes experiments to clarify points that aren't particularly obvious. Pick some short examples and experiment. Once you've got sysex equipment control working once you might even become enthusiastic about it.

But whatever you do, don't get too enthusiastic. Embedding sysex data inside your sequences will always render your sequences non-portable. In other words, when you change your equipment you'll need to completely re-write all the sysex control stuff!

Sysex control is useful to know about but, for what should now be fairly obvious reasons, it is not used extensively by the majority of Midi users. When sysex messages are needed, for example to set up controls on Midi units that cannot be accessed by conventional means, it usually needs to be done before the song sequence itself is played. My approach is to use a separate initial control sequence that contains all the preliminary program change messages along with a closed hi-hat count in. When necessary it is in this control sequence that I place any sysex messages, placing them as the first events of the sequence. That way I always know where to find them.

There are a collection of generally recognised sysex messages which have been developed for sampler data dump purposes. These incorporate optional handshaking commands which allow for error recovery, pauses when transmitting large amounts of data (to allow the receiving equipment to process the information), and so on.

General messages which enable Midi software to ask connected Midi units to identify themselves are also available. Unit replies are again done via sysex. These message facilities, since they are normally only of interest to Midi software developers, will not be discussed further. Interested readers should consult the official Midi Standard documentation.

13 Standard Midi Files

Despite the fact that Standard Midi Files have been about for quite a while there is, for many users, still more than a little confusion about their purpose and use. It's time to shed some light on the subject.

About four years ago I started to develop what some people would call an unhealthy interest in Standard Midi Files. More to the point I developed an interest in the problems that people were experiencing as they tried to understand and use them. Unlike the Midi Standard itself, on which much has been written, the Midi File is, for many, still surrounded in an air of mystery. It's not surprising, because for a long time details of the inner contents of these files were neither particularly easy to get hold of nor particularly easy to understand even if you did get hold of them.

Standard Midi Files (often called SMF files or just Midi Files) are used primarily to transfer time-stamped Midi data between different software packages. In other words they are computer disk files which have been created in such a way that other programs are able to read and understand their contents. Having this sort of data portability is obviously good news for Midi users because it means that they can change sequencers and change computers without having to worry about sequencer file compatibility problems. At least that's the way it should work.

Midi files have been around for quite a time and those of you who are established 'Midi-ites' will no doubt remember the many early Midi programs—such as Intelligent Music's Jam Factory and Steinberg's Pro 24—which lent their support to the idea of a common, portable file format. Today a great many software packages provide some level of Midi file support and more and more users are beginning to realize the benefits of such an arrangement.

Unfortunately, through the years things have gone rather less than smoothly on the Midi file development front and it's possible that early snags are partly to blame for many users still being rather suspicious of using them. To start with the file format initially proposed was limited to just a single stream of Midi data. This was felt by many software houses to be too restrictive and nowadays the Midi File standard, under the control of the International Midi Association, has grown to allow multiple streams, sequencer specific messages and a host of other goodies.

The penalty paid for these new benefits is that the standard has changed somewhat from that originally proposed. Most of these changes were to be expected and from a user viewpoint they have in the main been fairly transparent. Some transitional problems have however clearly been evident, and problems have come to light particularly when users have tried to read newer Midi files with packages which expected older style Midi files to be presented to them. When you add these type of problems to all the others that people encountered as they moved into the world of Midi then it's not surprising that many users didn't place learning about Midi files very high on their list of early priorities.

If as a Midi user you were new to computers and all of the related jargon then you had your work cut out anyway. Once happy with the computer related aspects of this new technology then Midi itself, and another load of jargon and technical oomph, had to be tackled.

Despite all these hurdles one would imagine, since we all cope with these learning curve problems one way or the other, that having tackled and used computers and Midi that the worst was over. Given time, surely a similar in-depth understanding of Midi files would follow? Sorry to disappoint you but for many users this was definitely not the case. Perhaps the best way to explain why this turned out to be so is by comparing the Midi File situation with that of Midi itself.

When you go out and buy, say, a Yamaha sound module you'll get a comprehensive manual which contains, amongst other things, a lot of technical Midi info. You'll learn not only how to use the beast from the front panel but also how the various remote Midi facilities and sysex control options can be used. One of the reasons you are provided with the manufacturer specific sysex information is that there is a general directive within the Midi specification for manufacturers to provide this type of information in their manuals.

Most do, and most make a very good job of it. Now, during the early days you might not make much sense out of all the technical material but the thing that's important is that this material is there if you need it. More to the point, if you hit some snag or want something explained in more detail all you have to do is write to Yamaha and it's 99.9% certain that they'll find a way to help you. And all of the other major musical equipment companies do likewise.

Many organisations have even issued introductory guides and books explaining what Midi is, how it can be used, and these include outlining the Midi standard and its purpose. The end result of all this is that becoming Midi-literate nowadays is relatively easy.

When you move into the Midi file arena, however, this situation changes drastically. Very few software companies will discuss internal details of their sequencer's Midi files, and are far from happy about discussing the sequencer specific events which many embed in such files, despite the fact that, like the Midi Standard itself, the Midi File standard includes a general directive to software companies to include such details.

Software companies in general, and this includes all software companies not just Midi and music related ones, are rather unhelpful. Most of the time they regard any such file format information as an area which is strictly private and do all they can to discourage you from delving too deeply into it. There are exceptions, of course, and companies like Dr T's for example do publish a certain amount of technical info about the file formats which they adopt.

So the trouble with Midi Files is quite simply that not enough has been written about them. If the same barriers had existed with Midi itself then there would have been a good chance that Midi would never have taken off in the way that it did.

My solution to this particular technical black hole—and I wouldn't recommend unless you have a lot of time available—was to sit down and, using the official standard as a guide, write my own Midi file diagnostic software. But before going any further there is something I need to point out.

I have quite deliberately included some rather technical file structure material. It's there to provide an anchor point for the things I want to discuss. If you've only just been introduced to Midi then don't be put off by how much there appears to learn. Just absorb what you can.

Making a Start

Midi Files, are designed to allow Midi data—your sequences, track data and songs—to be stored in a standardized way. Being able to take a sequencer file written by one sequencer and read it into another sequencer is good news because if you ever want to change your computer, change your sequencer, or perhaps write a song using two different sequencers, to take advantage of special effects for example, then this type of 'data portability' is extremely important.

Such portability, providing a standard file arrangement is available, should in theory be fairly straightforward, but problems can arise even before you get anywhere near the data itself. The first snag is the physical size of the disks you are using. Some dedicated sequencers use 'micro-floppies' whereas computer based sequencers tend to be either 5.25in or 3.5in. If you can't physically put the source disk into the new computer or sequencer you are using you'll be stuck before you even start. Equally important is the disk format which dictates the methods and arrangements by which datafiles are stored on the disk.

The two early solutions to this potential dilemma were to resort to copying the Midi data in real time—connecting the computers and sequencers with a Midi lead and playing one sequencer whilst recording with the other—or, if you were using computer based sequencers, transferring the data files using the computer serial ports, so-called serial transfer.

Linking two computers via their serial port connections is not hard but it's not really a suitable topic for this book. If you ever need to adopt this approach then either find yourself a friendly computer freak or use one of the many disk duplication companies who will copy your data onto new size/format disks.

Nowadays disk drives are quite flexible devices and many computers can read and write more than one type of disk format. This has eased many file transfer problems. Atari STs, for instance, can read PC disks. With a utility like Consultron's CrossDOS so can the Amiga. Moving Midi files between PC, ST and Amiga based sequencers using 3.5in disks is very easy indeed—you just shove the alien disk into the drive and your software will read it just as if it were a disk which had been written by the machine itself.

What you need to be aware of at this stage is this: None of the above jiggery pokery is specific to Midi Files as such, they are steps which would be taken to transfer any type of computer file—text, sound samples, graphics or even the computer programs themselves.

Enter the Midi File Proper

Before talking about some of the snags that can occur, there is yet another a technical hurdle to cope with. Just as it is not possible to discuss Midi without having some idea of the types of Midi messages which exist and the information they hold, so it isn't possible to discuss Midi files unless you know a bit about how they are built and the events they can contain.

If you are not yet at the 'Midi Techie' stage, don't worry if some of the following descriptions make little sense. Try however to develop a general understanding of the individual blocks of data held in such files, the events which the blocks contain and the fact that each event has an associated time value.

A Midi File, just like any other computer file, consists of a series of bytes. The Midi File standard specifies the interpretation and arrangement of those bytes. At the highest level Midi Files consist of identifiable blocks of data called chunks. Each chunk consists of a four-character identifier followed by a 32-bit number which specifies the byte-length of the data held in the chunk, so all chunks adopt the following type of arrangement...

| Chunk | <chunk-identifier> | <chunk-size> | <actual chunk data> |
| | 4 Bytes | 4 Bytes | chunk-size bytes |

Only two types of chunks are currently defined: Header chunks which have a 'MThd' identifier, and track chunks which have a 'MTrk' identifier. It is highly likely that new chunk types will cappear, so any programs which read SMF files have to assume that they will, one day, come across chunks which they cannot interpret.

The idea then, if you were writing your own software, would be to write programs which looked at the chunk identifiers and skipped over any chunks that couldn't be recognised.

Overall Chunk Arrangements

At the moment the two chunk types can be arranged in three ways and these lead to the three types of Midi files:

Format 0 type files contain a header chunk followed by a single track chunk. It's the simplest and most portable of all the Midi file arrangements and is used for storing a sequence as a single stream of events. This is a particularly useful format for performance oriented Midi File player programs, programs that have to read and play Midi Files in real-time.

Format 1 type files allow multiple simultaneous track sequences to be handled. These files will contain a header chunk followed by any number of separate track chunks.This format enables multiple-track based sequences to be moved to other sequencers keeping the track arrangements intact.

Format 2 files allow sets of independent sequences to be stored. A sequencer might save the individual sequences—verse, chorus and so on—which make up a complete song as a single Format 2 type Midi File. Figure 13.1 shows these file types graphically.

```
+++++++++++++          +++++++++++++

*** TRK 1 ***          *** TRK 1 ***

Type 0 files hold a single   *** TRK 2 ***
track of sequence data
                            *** TRK 3 ***


    +++    header chunk     Type 1 files hold chunks
    ***    track chunk      representing parallel track
                            information
```

```
+++++++++++++...*** SEQ 1 ***...*** SEQ 2 ***...*** SEQ 3 *** etc.

Type 2 files can handle sets of independent sequences by treating each
track chunk as a separate sequence
```

Figure 13.1: The three types of Midi files.

The Midi File standard guarantees that all Midi files will start with a header chunk, and that even if this header chunk is extended, existing fields will not be rearranged. Programs can therefore assume that even though they may find header chunks larger than they anticipated, the fields defined to date will remain in the same relative positions.

Header Chunks

As I've said, the MThd header chunk is always the first chunk in a Midi file. Like all chunks these start with the identifier followed by four bytes which specify the chunk's size. Current header chunks have six bytes of data. The first two bytes give the file format (0,1, or 2), the second two bytes tell you how many track chunks are present in the file, and the last two bytes contain timing division information. The contents therefore take the following form...

4 Bytes	'MThd' identifier
4 Bytes	Byte size of following data (currently 6)
2 Bytes	Midi file type (0, 1 or 2)
2 Bytes	Number of Tracks (always 1 for file type 0)
2 Bytes	division information

Interpretation-wise the only tricky item is the 'division' field because its contents and format may vary. Here are the details.

If bit 15, the most significant bit, is zero then bits 14-0 give a 15-bit number that specifies how many delta-time ticks make up a crotchet...

bit 15	bit 14 .... bit 0
0	Ticks per crotchet

If bit 15 is set to 1 it indicates that a time-code based time is being specified. In this case bits 14-8 give a negative number (two's complement) representing one of the four SMPTE or Midi Timecode formats: -24,-25, -29 (used for 30 drop frame) or -30. The second byte gives the resolution within the frame with typical values being 4, 8, 10, 80 or 100.

bit 15	bit 14 ...... bit 8	bit 7 ...... bit 0
1	Negative of the SMPTE format	Resolution

The bottom line as far as these header chunks are concerned is that they provide the software reading the file with some indication of the data which is to come. Your Midi data is packed into units known as track chunks and it is these arrangements that are the subject of the next chapter.

14 Track Chunks

In the last chapter I introduced the basic idea of the Standard Midi File and got as far as describing the Midi File header chunks. Now we need to document the chunks which hold, amongst other things, the Midi messages which your sequencer will have stored when you created a sequence or song.

Track chunks are the file sub-sections which hold the real file data. They consist of a four-byte track chunk identifier 'MTrk', a 32-bit length field which identifies how much data the chunk contains, and one or more MTrk events. The events themselves take a standardised form which starts with a time field that specifies the amount of time which should pass before the specified event occurs. These time fields, which are incidentally an integral part of the 'grammatical description' (syntax) of a Midi file event, are called 'delta times'. The name probably arose because delta is the Greek letter used by mathematicians to identify small numbers and small changes. Since the time gaps which occur between Midi file events represent relatively small time values the term delta time was adopted.

Like several other Midi File items, delta times are stored using a variable length format containing seven real bits per byte. The most significant bit (bit 7) is used to indicate either the continuation, or the end, of the possibly multibyte number...

1st byte	2nd byte ...	... nth byte
1xxx xxxx	1xxx xxxx ...	... 0xxx xxxx

The 1 indicates that more bytes are to follow

The 0 indicates the last byte of the number

Why such a complicated arrangement? It's simply to save space. Using this number form the inter-event times which are less than 128 (the majority of delta-times) can be stored using just a single byte. The number 127 for example can be stored as binary 0111 1111. Once the time value gets above 127 more bytes are needed to store the number.

Midi File events themselves can be one of three types: A Midi event, a sysex event, or something called a meta event. Midi events should already be familiar to you so I'll deal with these first.

Midi Events

Nowadays these are defined as being any Midi channel message. This implies that Midi files can only contain channel voice or channel mode Midi messages. In this respect the Midi file standard would seem to have changed because the early (pre IMA) standard used to allow storage of both channel messages and system common messages.

Sysex Events

Normal sysex messages use a modified form which includes an additional byte-count, field, stored as a variable length number.

Sysex Event1   <F0 hex> <length> <data bytes>

If the Sysex message is sent as a single packet then the last data byte should be the EOX (F7 hex) sysex terminator. This may appear to be unnecessary since a sysex message length field is also included. In the original Midi File standard it was indeed unnecessary and the terminal F7 byte was not required. The reason the F7 terminator has been reintroduced is that a new Midi file sysex message has been devised which allows large sysex messages to be broken down into time-stamped packets. The new message actually starts with the F7 hex terminator and takes this general form...

Sysex Event2   <F7> <length> <data bytes>

If you want to split a sysex message into time-stamped packets you can do it by using the F0 form for the first data packet, and F7 forms for any subsequent packets. The last data byte of the last packet of information containing a 'real' terminal F7 hex data byte. There is no requirement within the current Midi File Standard for this second message type to include an initial F0 hex sysex status byte. This means that it would be permissible, in theory, for non-legal Midi file Midi messages (such as Song Select, Song Position Pointer, real-time or MTC messages) to be embedded within this latter form of sysex message.

From a purely asthetic viewpoint I like this new broken packet sysex addition but I suspect that this is an area of the current standard that may lead to a number of compatibility problems. As usual, no one seems prepared to talk about such issues!

Meta Events

The current Midi File standard supports a number of 'non-Midi' events known as meta events. All of these start with an FF hex character as the primary meta-event identifier and this is followed by a meta event 'type' field, a byte count, and finally the data itself.

Meta Event   <FF hex> <meta-event type> <length> <data bytes>

The meta-event type field is a 1 byte value between 0 and 127 and the length field is stored in the same variable length format as is used for delta-time values. In a sense the type field byte performs the same job as a Midi status byte but it is of course being used to classify an event type not a Midi message type.

The following table is given only for completeness. It provides a brief summary of the meta events currently defined, their formats and their contents. Amongst the meta events types are some variations of the basic text event which are used to identify particular types of ASCII text messages. Meta event type identifiers 02 hex to 0F hex have been reserved for such messages, although not all have been defined at the current time.

Description	Type (Hex)	Length	Details
Sequence No.	00	2	16-bit number representing a sequence number. Must occur at the start of the track, before any non-zero delta-times.
Text Event	01	variable	Text describing anything at all.
Copyright Notice	2	variable	Should be the first event in the first track.
Sequence or	03	variable	Another ASCII text eventTrack Name
Instrument Name	04	variable	An indication of the instrumentaton to be used for a track. It can be used in conjunction with a Prefix event to specify which Midi channel the description applies to, or the channel number can be specified within the text itself.
Lyric	05	variable	A lyric to be sung. The idea here is that each syllable will be a separate lyric event which is to begin at the event's starting time.
Marker	06	variable	Used to mark a specific point in a sequence.
Cue Point	07	variable	A marker event used for video/film cue point marking.
	08 - 0F		Reserved, but currently undefined.

Channel Prefix	20	1	Contains a single data byte which associates subsequent events with a particular Midi channel. This state is effective until the next normal Midi event, or the next Channel Prefix event.
End Of Track	2F	0	This event *must* be used so that an exact ending point can be specified for a track. It's use is not optional!
Set Tempo	51	3	A 24-bit number which represents microseconds per quarter note. These events should really only occur at positions where real Midi clocks would be located.
SMPTE Offset	54	5	The five bytes of this message indicate hours, minutes, seconds frame and frame fraction (in 1/100th's of a frame).
Time Signature	58	4	The time signature is expressed as four numbers: NN, DD, CC, and BB. NN is the time signature numerator, DD is the denominator expressed as a power of 2, CC is the number of Midi clocks in a metronome click, and BB represents the number of 32nd notes in a Midi quarter note.
Sequencer Specific	7F	variable	This event allows sequencers to include their own sequencer specific info. Manufacturers who use such events are *supposed* to publish the formats so that others can interpret them.

Last Words

That then is the basis of the current Midi file standard as adopted by the International Midi Association. It's worth mentioning that running status (the use of implied status bytes) is also allowed within a stream of Midi events but this must not be carried across non-channel events. If a stream of running status Midi messages are interrupted by one or more meta or sysex events then a new status byte must be present in the first of anyMidi messages which follow.

To my mind at least it is evident that several changes have occured which may make Midi files written with early sequencer programs incompatible with sequencers designed to read and write the current standard. If nothing else this might be a useful warning for many people who seem to believe that early Midi files are equivalent to the new type 0 Midi files. Whilst similar, they are clearly *not* identical.

The end-of-track events, which used to be optional, must now always be present. Set Tempo and Time Signature meta-events have changed size, sysex messages have been re-defined, and a variety of new meta-events have been proposed. There are now explicitly defined header and track chunks, and of course system common messages are no longer allowed. The standard was officially published in July 1988, so presumably if you are still using software packages which support Midi files but which were released before this time there's a good chance that they will not be implementing the full IMA adopted standard.

15 Some Parting Advice

Once you get into Midi the chance of you not buying extra equipment, or changing some existing item, is remote. Midi is addictive and the ease with which you can link new gear to your existing set up makes such growth tempting to say the least. Despite the fact that most of the new 'toys' that can be added— expanders, extra drum machines, alternative sequencers and so on—will be trouble free, there are some less-than-well-known snags worth mentioning...

With the early generation of drum machines, for instance, each drum had a fixed Midi note-number and these correspondences were fixed. Originally many hoped that an early common standard would be adopted so that Yamaha's bass drum notes would be the same as Roland's, which would be the same as Casio's and so on. This didn't happen. But the problems were eased because most professional sequencers offered drum-note remapping facilities to ease the burden of translating drum parts from one set of drum/note-number correspondences to another.

Whilst this drum part remapping idea is fine when you have only a few songs and sequences to change, most established Midi musicians end up with song libraries containing hundreds of songs, each of which contain many different sequences. Because of the time it takes, having to sit down and change every song in such a library is an absolute nightmare. The newer generation of drum machines, such as the Yamaha RX8, opted for user-assignable drum/note-number correspondences. These type of units can be configured so that the new drum/note number correspondences match the existing drum note relationships of your stored sequence data. Reconfiguring a drum machine like the Yamaha RX8 takes only a few minutes and this approach avoids having to edit your existing song data.

General Midi and Roland's GS standards have now tackled these issues. So if this problem has been solved, why bring it up again? There are a variety of reasons: Firstly, although General Midi is here it will be a long time before everyone is using GM/GS equipment exclusively, and even once all new equipment supports these new guidelines there'll still be the previous generation of equipment around. Even today there are masses of the early fixed drum/note-number percussion units (Yamaha's RX21 and RX21L models are two that come to mind) readily available on the second-hand market. Whilst there's no doubt that these do offer a cheap way of adding extra percussion facilities, you need to be careful.

The main danger is that some of the drum note correspondences will clash with the assignments you've already adopted. It is an easy danger to avoid. Before you opt for adding any such unit, check the manual and the implementation chart to see that the drum note values do not clash with anything you are using already.

The second reason I mentioned the drum machine problem is to drive home a point which will become increasingly important as your Midi work progresses. When only a few dozen songs are involved, going through each sequence and making various edit changes is not that time consuming. After a few years of arranging and collecting Midi sequence data though your library is likely to have grown to the point where these type of manual global-edit operations are no longer feasible because of the time they would take.

Problems can of course also appear when you change or add synthesizers and additional sound modules. You are bound to want many of your existing sequences to sound much the same as they did originally, so to start with voices on the new unit must be found that correspond to the voices available on the previous equipment. This will entail finding (and possibly creating) the appropriate voices and making sure that the new voices are used.

As we've seen, voice selection is usually done via Midi program change commands and these messages will of course be embedded in your sequences. If, for example, a progam change 23 had selected a cello voice on your Roland HS10, then you'll need to be able to make any new unit select a equivalent voice when it receives a program change 23 command.

One of the most important facilities on any new synthesizer units that you buy will be some form of user-definable program change table. This will let you assign any voice to any program change number, and so in this way you'll be able to avoid having to edit any of your existing sequence data. In short you create or find the required voices on the new unit and then set up the program change table so that program numbers which are already embedded in your existing sequencer select appropriate voices in the new unit.

Sysex messages are an obvious difficulty as far as sequence portability is concerned. With expander units like Yamaha's TX81Z, which has quite a sophisticated set of sysex control messages, it's possible to do all sorts of clever tricks, for example create control sequences which modify the program change table just prior to the start of the real music sequence so that an alternative set of voices are made available. The facilities are brilliant—until the time comes when you change expanders and realize that all your clever sysex stuff is going to have to be completely rewritten. My advice? Certainly experiment and learn about sysex messages but do keep in the back of your mind the pitfalls of embedding this type of data in your sequences.

Midi controllers are another area to watch for. Problems in this area are minimized firstly by sticking to controllers which have a de facto standard usage and secondly by opting for new units which provide user-assignable controller functions. There's a good chance that more and more budget priced Midi equipment will include assignable controllers as the trend for increased programmability increases. Again, take a good look at the implementation sheet before you buy and check that none of the controller messages already present in your sequences will cause problems with the new equipment. Most sequencers will let you re-assign embedded controller numbers, but ideally you should aim to avoid placing yourself in a position where it becomes necessary to edit/remap controller numbers in all of your existing sequences.

Many of these troubles can be avoided by a bit of advance planning and the bottom line is this: Before you buy any new or second-hand Midi equipment, check the implementation sheets, looking carefully for potential areas of incompatibility with the information you've built up during your Midi lifetime. Look for flexibility in the areas of program change tables and Midi controller assignability, and identify controller number conflicts before you commit yourself to a new Midi unit. Above all, avoid unnecessary dependence on sysex control messages because they are equipment specific and will cause serious portability problems if embedded in sequence data.

I've shifted hundreds of songs across to new sequencers and have used these song arrangements with a wide range of Midi synthesizers, expanders, drum machines and effects units. The one thing that has really been driven home to me is that the key issue in such transfers is to find out how to avoid having to undertake any major editing of the existing sequence data!

Last of all—which you should note but keep in perspective—comes the big one: changing sequencers. If you change from a dedicated sequencer, such as the Alesis MMT-8, to a computer/software based sequencer package like an Atari Falcon running Steinberg's Cubase or an Amiga running Dr T's KCS, then the safest way of moving your sequencer files can often be to do it in real-time. Connect the two sequencers and play one whilst you record with the other.

Don't forget that the sequencer which you're recording into should be set so that it is using the Midi clock messages and not any internal clock, otherwise you'll lose all of your existing bar definitions. This method of direct linking is simple to do, and even though it can take time it has one overriding advantage—it always works! If you've already got a computer based sequencer then there are other possibilities. If the file formats of the two sequencers are compatible it may be possible, via a serial comms package or self written software, to transmit the sequencer files from one machine to the other directly. Alternatively use Standard Midi Files.

Please keep things in perspective. Once you have a little Midi literacy and some practical experience under your belt, Midi becomes virtually trouble free. So don't too get hung up on the complexity issues and the sometimes imagined pitfalls—unless you enjoy that side of things.

Above all Midi should be about making and enjoying music. It should be fun, but do bear in mind that the more you learn about Midi in general, the more you'll get out of it.

Appendix 1 Hexadecimal Numbers

In the decimal number system 10 different symbols (the digits 0-9 inclusive) are used to represent numbers. Each digit in a number is 10 times more significant than the digit to its right, and ten times less significant than the digit to its left. This '10 times' relationship that exists between the digits of all decimal numbers is obviously a fundamental part of the decimal numbering system. If, for example, we consider the number 374 and write a full description of what each digit means we can see that it is just a convenient way of expressing this sum...

$(3 \times 100) + (7 \times 10) + 4$

Going one better than this, and bearing in mind that any number raised to the power zero is unity, you can express each effective digit term as a product of one digit and a power of 10, like this...

$3 \times 10^2 + 7 \times 10^1 + 1 \times 10^0$

For decimal numbers, 10 is known as the 'radix' or base of the numbering system. Many other bases are possible. Computers use binary—base 2 numbers which consist of strings of 0s and 1s. Again, if you think of a binary number in terms of its explicit radix = 2 representation it's easy to see the relationship between the binary and decimal number systems...

$$1011 \text{ binary } = \quad 1 \times 2^3 + 0 \times 2^2 + 1 \times 2^1 + 1 \times 2^0$$
$$8 \quad + \quad 0 \quad + \quad 2 \quad + \quad 1 \quad = 11 \text{ decimal}$$

By writing out what the binary number means in full it becomes quite easy to see that 1011 binary is the decimal number 11.

Computers use binary numbers internally because the two digits 0 and 1 relate directly to the possible states of bits within the memory hardware. Binary numbers are intimately involved with a great many computing applications, but since they are not that easy for us humans to work with (because long strings of 0s and 1s are easily misinterpreted) a related radix scheme is often used as an alternative.

Hexadecimal numbers use a radix of 16, and the 16 symbols used are the digits 0-9 plus the letters A-F. Each column in a base 16 number represents some power of the base. For example the decimal number 16 itself is written as 10 hex, because...

$$10 \ \text{hex} = \quad 1 \times 16^1 + 0 \times 16^0$$
$$16 \quad + \quad 0 \quad = 16 \ \text{decimal}$$

$$1F \ \text{hex} = \quad 1 \times 16^1 + 15 \times 16^0$$
$$16 \quad + \quad 15 \quad = 31 \ \text{decimal}$$

The fact that the bases of the binary and hexadecimal numbering systems are power related (2 to the power of 4 equals 16) produces a special and very useful relationship between these two numbering systems—it allows one hexadecimal digit to represent *four* binary digits. Best of all the binary-to-hex conversion process is very easy to understand once you've learnt the following table.

binary	hex	binary	hex
0000	0	1000	8
0001	1	1001	9
0010	2	1010	A
0011	3	1011	B
0100	4	1100	C
0101	5	1101	D
0110	6	1110	E
0111	7	1111	F

To convert a hexadecimal number into binary form you just replace each hexadecimal digit with its group of four binary digits. To convert a binary number to its hex form you peel off (from right to left) groups of four bits and replace them with the corresponding hex digit. So to convert CF hex to the binary equivalent you'd replace each of the two hexadecimal symbols with the binary equivalents like this...

```
CF hex =  C       F
          1100    1111  = 11001111 binary
```

To go the other way you take groups of four bits from the binary number and replace then with the corresponding hex digits. The binary number 1111000010101010, for example, could be translated to hexadecimal form as follows...

```
1111000010101010 =  1111  0000  1010  1010
                    F     0     A     A = F0AA hex
```

Using and converting between binary, hex and decimal number systems is not that difficult but it does take practice. Familiarity with hex and binary number forms is also essential for understanding how the bitwise logical operations provided by most high-level languages work. In Midi-oriented computer programs you often need to perform logical AND and OR operations which are based on these two truth tables...

X	Y	X AND Y	
0	0	0	
1	0	0	Logical AND Operation
0	1	0	
1	1	1	

X	Y	X OR Y	
0	0	0	
1	0	1	Logical OR Operation
0	1	1	
1	1	1	

Being able to picture in your mind what these tables mean is a big advantage. If you AND two operands together then only the bit positions where both operands have a bit set to 1 will produce a 1 in the result. With the OR operation you'll get a 1 in the result when either (or both) of the bits in that position in the corresponding operands are set to 1. The bit pattern for F0 hex for instance is 11110000 so ANDing any value with F0 hex will force the lower four bits of the result to zero - the value F0 hex is called a mask because it masks out certain bit positions.You'll find examples of this type of use in these appendices. The OR operation is also useful because it can force bit positions to take particular values. You'll find an example where a Midi channel number is combined with a general Midi message code to create a complete status byte.

One last thing. Most Basics require hex numbers to be identified by using an &H prefix. So in Basic F0 hex would be written as &HF0, FAA hex would be &HFAA, and so on.

Appendix 2 Notes For Hackers

For non General Midi users some sequence editing is usually required when using other people's sequences. Similarly a change in synthesizer, or addition of a new expander unit, can also mean that a few program change numbers or controller values then need to be altered in your own sequences. Most users are able to do these sort of things directly from their sequencers but there are times however when, because of either sequencer editing limitations or because of the sheer number of sequences involved, alternative approaches needed to be found.

Suppose someone gives you some disks containing hundreds of sequences but in order to use them you need to perform global editing operations on *all* of the drum notes held in the sequences.

Now some sequencers do provide easy to use drum part remapping facilities. Other sequencers offer no help at all but few sequencers allow you to perform easy automated global edits on batches of sequence files. Editing sequences using the one-by-one approach required by most sequencer programs can take a lot of time.

Even drum units that offer user-definable drum assignments do not particularly help because building and using a library of song data which contains files based on a variety of note-drum correspondences is a nightmare (and so an option best forgotten about). In trying to solve problems like this we enter the domain of the true Midi hacker - the expert who can solve any editing or portability problem that comes along!

I've talked about various aspects of Midi/music related standards and file structures but have deliberately kept well clear of any mention of proprietary file structures, the sequencer-specific internal formats used by sequencer manufacturers. It's worth knowing however that the structures of many of these internal formats are relatively simple. This means that the job of writing a utility to perform some specific editing of an internal sequencer file format is usually much easier than writing say a generalised Midi file event editor. Very occasionally sequencing snags can arise in which the easiest solution is to write your own sequence editing software.

Direct remapping of drum parts when large numbers of sequences are involved is one obvious case which comes to mind. As we've seen earlier, many drum machines differ in both the types of drum sounds they produce and, more importantly, in the note-drum assignments they use. If you send a Yamaha RX21 drum unit a C4 Midi note it will play a crash cymbal but the same note sent to play percussion on a Roland MT32 unit produces a High Bongo. If you have sequences which had been written with an RX21 in mind then you've got some drum note translation work to do before those sequences will be of any use with an MT32 based Midi set up. In this appendix I want to sketch out the ideas behind a typical hackers edit program that will automate these types of translations.

Writing your own file modification utility might seem like a last resort approach, but once you have understood the principles involved you'll realise that all such programs follow a similar pattern. This means that once you've written one such utility, other related programs will be quite straightforward to create. In fact, if you stick to creating short utilities which do specific jobs, rather than trying to write all-singing-all-dancing versions which cater for more general editing possibilities, you'll be surprised how easy and quick it is.

I'm talking here about programs then that are similar to the sort of hack utilities that coders write for stripping out linefeeds, removing control characters from word-processor files and so on. In other words, cheap and cheerful, easily written command line utilities that can be knocked out by most programmers within half an hour or so. The aim is not to win coding prizes, it's just to get the job done with the minimum of effort.

The basic plan for the drum translation program is simple. Firstly, the data file has to be read into a buffer. Secondly, all the notes of the designated drum channel have to be identified and changed to the new values. Lastly, the modified file has to be saved back to disk. Usually the biggest problem as far as Midi sequences are concerned is getting the sequencer file format information in the first place. Given sufficient time, and the right combination of luck and common-sense, I suppose it is just possible to hack your way into the file structure and build up a picture of how the data is stored. Unless you either enjoy such pastimes, or it looks to be the only way to get the necessary information, this pathway is not to be recommended. The best first step is usually to contact the company concerned, explain exactly what you are trying to do and why, and see whether they have a policy of releasing details of their internal file layouts.

A few years ago I had to find a way of converting a lot of SEQ type Dr T's KCS sequences that had been written for an old Yamaha RX21 machine so that they played properly on a drum unit that used the Roland MT32 scheme. This was in the days long before the MPE-oriented level II Dr T's KCS with the PVG/master editor program became available. (OK affordable.) Drum part remapping on the basic KCS sequencer, though possible, was not particularly easy.

At this time I contacted Dr T's in the States and asked for details of their KCS SEQ sequence files. Back came the reply with the necessary details: Firstly, an SEQ file has a 14-byte file header arrangement...

2 bytes.	An ID value
4 bytes	Number of events in the file
8 bytes.	Sequence name

After the header comes the list of events. Each event was six bytes long and those which were of interest were the ones which turned notes on. The format was as follows...

2 byte	event-time	
1 byte	event-type	
1 byte	note-value	bits used
1 byte	note-velocity	7 bits used
1 byte	note-duration	10 bits used

The event-time didn't concern me. Event-type for a note-on event turns out to be a Midi note-on status byte. The remaining three bytes were a bit more tricky. Note and velocity data values only need seven bits, so the high bits of these bytes are used to store a couple of extra note-duration bits, the duration is actually stored as a 'broken' 10-bit field.

The remapping utility would therefore have to operate like this: The file would have to be read into memory, then the header's event count would need to be looked at to see how many events were involved. Having done that, the program would have to look at each event and for each note-on event on the right Midi channel, convert the existing note value to the required new value. Before converting a note, bit 7 had to be checked to see if it was set. If it was it had to be preserved so that the event's duration was not inadvertently changed.

The example program that follows is the code that I knocked up to do this conversion. You'll see that I've defined header and event structures based on the SEQ file details. The use of C structures to mirror the inherent file structure helps to keep the code uncluttered. It makes it easy to move from one event to another and it also lets me reference chosen fields within any given event in a tidy fashion, so that I don't have to play around adding strange offsets to pointers in order to reference the bytes I wish to look at.

A note table is used to perform the Yamaha RX21-to-Roland MT32 conversion. Since the MT32 has more drums than the RX21 I had to decide on a suitable MT32 drum sub-set to use and the correspondences that I opted for were these...

DRUM	*RX21 NOTE*	*CHOSEN MT32 CONVERTED NOTE*
Bass Drum	45	35
Tom 3	48	43
Tom 2	50	45
Snare	52	8
Tom 1	53	48
HandClap	54	39
Closed Hi-hat	57	42
Open Hi-hat	59	46
Crash Cymbal	60	49

In the program that follows you'll see these Midi note values set up in a *note_table[]* array and it's this that would have needed to be altered had I wished to produce some alternative remapping arrangements. This particular utility was written for the Amiga but the general code arrangements would be similar on any other computer. It's just the *LoadBuffer()* and *SaveBuffer()* routines, which use some Amiga-specific functions, that would need to be modified.

To use the resulting program all I had to type was the program name, the source sequence name, and the destination sequence name parameters. For example, this command line...

```
REMAP DF0:TEST.SEQ RAM:MODIFIED.SEQ
```

would read the file TEST.SEQ into memory, make the required conversions, and then write the modified data as a file called MODIFIED.SEQ into the ram-disk device. Coupled with the Lattice C (Now SAS C) build/extract utilities it was easy to create a script file which automatically used my converter program to edit a whole batch of sequencer files. Once the .SEQ file content details were available from Dr T this program took less than an hour to plan, write, compile, link, and test. Fifteen minutes later all my sequences (about 180 of them) had been converted to work with the new drummer.

Now this example concerned drum part remapping but obviously the basic ideas can be used to create programs capable of editing any number of event characteristics. Similar programs can be written to directly alter standard Midi files but, because of the more complicated file structures, the programming does get rather more involved.

```
/* ================================================================ */
/* Title: Simple Midi note remapping utility to get you thinking    */
/* ---------------------------------------------------------------- */

/* some defines... */

#define BUFFERSIZE 10000

#define EVENT_TYPE 0x99

/* This program is a hack not a general utility and in this example
we're looking ONLY for notes on MIDI channel 10 hence... the EVENT_TYPE
shown above is a channel 10 NOTE-ON status byte */

/* some includes... */

#include <exec/types.h>

#include <exec/memory.h>

#include <libraries/dos.h>
```

```
/* some prototypes... */
BOOL LoadBuffer(TEXT *, UBYTE *, LONG);
BOOL SaveBuffer(TEXT *, UBYTE *, ULONG);
struct FileHandle *Open(TEXT *, ULONG);
/* some structure definitions... */
struct Header {
    UWORD SequenceID;
    ULONG EventCount;
    UBYTE SequenceName[8];
};
struct Event {
    UWORD Time;
    UBYTE Type;
    UBYTE Note;
    UBYTE Velocity;
    UBYTE Duration;
};
/* some globals... */
UBYTE  buffer[BUFFERSIZE]; /* Sequence data buffer */
UBYTE  note_table[128];    /* Note conversion table */
struct Header *header;
struct Event  *event;
/* ------------------------------------------------------------------ */
main(int argc, char *argv[])
{
UCOUNT i;
/* The  note_table[] array contains changes that are to be made to the
existing drum assignments. The i'th element of the array holds the new
value for a note of value 'i'. Notes whose values are to be left
unchanged are simply re-assigned as the same value. */
/* Do a 'no change' initialisation... */
for (i=0;i<128;i++){note_table[i]=i;}
```

```
/* Set up values to be remapped... */
note_table[45]=35; /* BASS DRUM */
note_table[48]=43; /* TOM-3 DRUM */
note_table[50]=45; /* TOM-2 DRUM */
note_table[52]=38; /* SNARE DRUM */
note_table[53]=50; /* TOM-1 DRUM */
note_table[54]=39; /* HAND CLAP */
note_table[57]=42; /* CLOSED HI-HAT */
note_table[59]=46; /* OPEN HI-HAT */
note_table[60]=49; /* CRASH CYMBAL */
if(argc>2)
    {
/* user has given source and destination filenames so start by trying
to load source file... */
    if(LoadBuffer(argv[1], buffer, BUFFERSIZE)==FALSE)
        {
/* File found so set up structure pointers... */
        header=(struct Header *)buffer;
        event=(struct Event *)(buffer+sizeof(struct Header));
/* Can't be sure that this really is a .SEQ file so it would be
safest if a check was made. For now though I'll assume that the user
knows what they're doing. We now need to look at each event to see
what type it is. If it is the type to be converted we must look to
see whether the high-bits need preserving. I've opted for an 'if high
then reset to high' approach because it's an easy way to ensure that
the seven bit note value gets replaced with the value held in the
note_table[] array */
        for(i=0;i<header->EventCount;i++) /* FOR EACH EVENT      */
            {
            if (event->Type==EVENT_TYPE) /* OF THE RIGHT TYPE  */
                {
                if (event->Type&0x80)      /* LOOK AT BIT 7      */
```

```
        {               /* BIT 7 SET SO MUST PRESERVE IT */
        event->Note=note_table[event->Note]|0x80;
        }
   else    {    /* BIT 7 NOT SET SO COPY STRAIGHT  */
        event->Note=note_table[event->Note];
        }
   } /* End of if (event->Type... TEST */
   event++; /* Do next event */
   } /* End of for (i=0.... LOOP */
```
/* All events in the file have been dealt with so we now save
the modified data using the filename specified by the 3rd CLI
argument... */
```
   SaveBuffer(argv[2], buffer, sizeof(struct Header)+header
->EventCount*sizeof(struct Event));
   } /* End of if(LoadBuffer... */
  } /* End of if(argc>1) */
} /* End of main() program */


/* ================================================================= */
/* Title:          LoadBuffer()                                      */
/* --------------------------------------------------------------- */
/* Takes an AmigaDos filename and attempts to open and load file    */
/* into specified buffer.  Only ONE error condition is returned and */
/* this can result from being unable to open the file, being unable */
/* to read it, or from finding that file is too large for the buffer.*/
/* --------------------------------------------------------------- */
BOOL LoadBuffer(TEXT *filename, UBYTE *buffer_p, LONG buffersize)
{
struct FileHandle *fh;
BOOL error_flag=FALSE;
if((fh=Open(filename, MODE_OLDFILE))==NULL) error_flag=TRUE;
```

```
     else {
          if(Read(fh,buffer_p,buffersize)<0) error_flag=TRUE;
          Close(fh);
          }
return(error_flag);
}


/* ================================================================ */
/* Title:           SaveBuffer()                                    */
/* ---------------------------------------------------------------- */
/* This routine will take an AmigaDos filename and attempt to create */
/* the file using data in specified buffer. Only ONE error condition */
/* is returned (error_flag=TRUE).                                   */
/* ---------------------------------------------------------------- */
BOOL SaveBuffer(TEXT *filename, UBYTE *buffer_p, ULONG data_size)
{
struct FileHandle *fh;
BOOL error_flag=FALSE;
LONG length;
if((fh=Open(filename, MODE_NEWFILE))==NULL) error_flag=TRUE;
   else {
          length=Write(fh,buffer_p,data_size);
          if(length<0) error_flag=TRUE;
          Close(fh);
          }
return(error_flag);
}
```

Appendix 3 Even Basic Can Do

Real-time Midi programming, such as is required to create a sequencer, can be difficult. Accurate time-stamping of events may mean getting involved with low-level serial port control and other system nasties. Believe it or not though, there are many useful Midi diagnostic utilities that can be written with just a few lines of Basic, and what I want to do in this appendix is provide some explanations of a few fundamental ideas which all Basic programmers will be able to get something useful out of. The example programs are not particularly complicated, although they do require a working familiarity with both binary/hexadecimal number conversion and bit-oriented AND/OR operations.

For the examples themselves I've chosen to use HiSoft Basic which is similar to many other Microsoft flavoured Basics including QuickBasic 3, which is available on PC based machines. HiSoft Basic itself is supported on the Amiga, Atari ST and Falcon machines, and although the Atari machines require the programmer to adopt a different approach for Midi port access, the underlying ideas that I'm going to discuss should be of use to programmers working with any Microsoft styled Basic on any machine.

I've chosen to use code written for the Amiga, and on this machine Midi serial port access can be achieved using the Amiga's SER: device—which means that the complexities of accessing the underlying Amiga serial port are transparent. All the programmer has to remember is that Preferences needs to be used to set suitable serial port characteristics,—a baud rate of 31250 with no parity, no handshaking, and just one stop bit.

The file handling approach of HiSoft Basic, and most other Basics come to that, is straightforward. The sequential file handling input/output conventions are that you output TO a file or input FROM a file, and so to open the Amiga's serial device for sending serial data this statement could be used...

```
OPEN "SER:" FOR OUTPUT AS #1
```

It turns out however that in order to make sure that Midi data is sent straightaway (and not buffered) it is better to explicitly set a buffer size of 1 byte. This modified form does the job...

```
OPEN "SER:" FOR OUTPUT AS #1 LEN=1
```

Once the serial device is open all that is needed is a way of sending Midi messages. The easiest way to transmit bytes of Midi information is to place them in a string variable or string expression. Supposing, for example, that I wished to transmit a Midi real-time stop message, which is a single byte whose value is decimal 252, FC hex. The CHR$() function can convert the decimal 252 numeric argument into a 1-byte character string and this can then be used in conjunction with Basic's PRINT# statement like this...

```
PRINT# 1, CHR$(252);
```

The result? A Midi stop message will be transmitted. Note that the semi-colon at the end of the statement prevents Basic from transmitting a newline character.

There are several ways of transmitting longer messages but the easiest approach is just to build up the messages using CHR$() coupled with Basic's string concatenation operator (+). To transmit a two byte program change message for example we send a program change status byte followed by the patch number. The general layout for a channel-n/patch-p message, as you'll know from earlier material, takes this form...

Status byte	*Data byte*
1100 nnnn binary	pppp pppp binary

Providing that we remember that Midi channel numbers 1-16 are actually transmitted as the numbers 0-15 and patch commands 1-128 are similarly represented by the numbers 0-127 it is easy to work out what bytes need to be transmitted. If, for example, we wanted to transmit a patch number = 6 command on Midi channel 2 we'd need to incorporate the numbers 5 and 1 respectively into the general message just described. The binary, hex, and decimal forms of the required numbers are as follows...

Status Byte	*Data Byte*
Prog Change Channel	Patch Number
1100 0001 binary	0000 0101 binary
C 1 hex	0 5 hex
193 decimal	5 decimal

And so the message which needs to be transmitted is this...

```
PRINT# 1, CHR$(193) + CHR$(5);
```

Most Midi programmers prefer to use hex values for status bytes and, in the above case, this would be done by re-writing the fragment as...

```
PRINT# 1, CHR$(&HC1) + CHR$(5);
```

Why use hex? Because working out decimal values for the status bytes is not only a pain but it also makes it harder to see what the status byte represents. The 1 value in the above status byte C1 hex tells you immediately that the byte refers to a channel 2 Midi message, and once you are Midi literate the C tells you that the status byte refers to a program change message. The same pieces of information are undoubtedly still there when the status byte is in decimal form, but neither the message type nor the channel number are particularly obvious.

A useful idea, as far as constant values are concerned, is to isolate the characters being transmitted so that they are no longer clutter the main program code. One way of doing this is to place required definitions at the start program. The definition written initially as...

```
REM define Midi message...
message$=CHR$(&HC1) + CHR$(4)
```

... might, for instance, be used later in the program as...

```
PRINT# 1, message$;
```

You don't have to use constant values in the PRINT# expressions. To send a two byte message consisting of the numerical values X and Y we could use something along the lines of...

```
PRINT# 1, CHR$(X) + CHR$(Y);
```

If we used X=&HCl and Y=5 then the same program change message as described earlier would be transmitted.

The variable approach is very useful when used as part of a Basic FOR/NEXT loop. To send all 128 channel program change messages on Midi channel 3 I could use a loop like this...

```
X=&HC2
FOR Y=0 to 127
  PRINT# 1, CHR$(X) + CHR$(Y);
NEXT Y
```

On the other hand, to send the program change patch 5 message on all 16 Midi channels I'd use a loop which modified the status byte value...

```
FOR X = &HCO TO &HCF
  PRINT# 1, CHR$(X) + CHR$(4);
NEXT X
```

This is fine for illustration purposes but in general it is better to use meaningful variables names. For example, in a real Midi program a twin loop that sent all program change number on all channels might then be written as something like...

```
FOR STATUS = &HCO TO &HCF
   FOR PATCH = 0 to 127
        PRINT# 1, CHR$(STATUS) + CHR$(PATCH);
   NEXT PATCH
NEXT STATUS
```

As well as binary-to-hex-to-decimal conversion, all potential Midi programmers also need to be confident about extracting part-values from a byte. Given a channel message status byte, for instance, you'll often need to be able to identify the channel and the message type. Channel numbers can be obtained from a status byte by masking out the upper four bits of a byte by ANDing with &HF, like this...

```
channel=ASC(status$) AND &HF
```

Similarly, masking out the lower four bits by ANDing with &HF0 will give the isolated Midi message class in the top four bits of the number...

```
messagetype=ASC(status$) AND &HF0
```

Sometimes the alternative situation will occur and you'll want to build up a status byte from the channel and message type values. In this case the values need to be combined by ORing. So to create and send a Note-On status byte we would logically OR &H90 with the channel number and transmit the value using this type of code...

```
PRINT# 1,CHR$(&H90 OR channel);
```

To transmit a complete note-on message we'd follow the status byte with a note number and a velocity value...

```
PRINT# 1,CHR$(&H90 OR channel)+CHR$(note)+CHR$(velocity);
```

The string part of these types of fragments are generally useful and easily turned into user-defined functions. Here's one which sends a complete Midi note-on message on a specified channel, this time using a fixed velocity value of 64...

```
DEF FNNoteOn$(note,ch)=CHR$(&H90 OR (ch-1))+CHR$(note)+CHR$(64)
```

Subtracting one from the channel number is a convenient for the program user, it allows them to work with conventional 1-16 channel numbers rather than the internal representations (0-15) that are needed by the program itself. Here's the alternative function to turn a note off...

```
DEF FNNoteOff$(note,ch)=CHR$(&H80 OR (ch-1))+CHR$(note)+CHR$(64)
```

It is possible to use these functions in all manner of ways. I could for example use data statements to define chords by adopting the convention that my data statements consisted of a note count followed by the values of the harmony intervals from some unspecified root note.

Chord descriptions could then be built up like this...

```
MajorChord: DATA 3,0,4,7 : REM three notes - root, mjr 3rd, perfect 5th
MinorChord: DATA 3,0,3,7 : REM three notes - root, mnr 3rd, perfect 5th
```

... and it is then possible to write a subprogram to play the notes of a given chord on a specified Midi channel...

```
SUB PlayChord(type$,rootnote,channel) STATIC
   IF type$="major" THEN RESTORE MajorChord
   IF type$="minor" THEN RESTORE MinorChord
   READ count
   FOR I= 1 TO count
        READ interval
        PRINT#1,FNNoteOn$(rootnote+interval,channel)
   NEXT I
END SUB
```

In the next listing I've put all these ideas into an example program which asks the user to provide a Midi channel value, and then plays a major C chord (with a middle C root) on that channel. When the left mouse button is pressed the major chord is cancelled and changed to C minor, and when the left mouse button is pressed again that minor chord is also cancelled. Not by any stretch of the imagination what you'd call a stunning Midi program but it does illustrate how all these ideas fit together in a real program.

```
REM -----------------------------------------------------------------
REM Some useful user-defined functions...
DEF FNNoteOn$(note,ch)=CHR$(&H90 OR (ch-1))+CHR$(note)+CHR$(64)
DEF FNNoteOff$(note,ch)=CHR$(&H80 OR (ch-1))+CHR$(note)+CHR$(64)
REM Constants...
MajorChord: DATA 3,0,4,7
MinorChord: DATA 3,0,3,7
root=60
REM -----------------------------------------------------------------
REM Main section of program code...
OPEN "SER:" FOR OUTPUT AS 1 LEN=1
INPUT "Please enter required Midi channel ";channel
CALL PlayChord("major",root,channel): GOSUB CheckMouse
CALL CancelChord("major",root,channel)
CALL PlayChord("minor",root,channel): GOSUB CheckMouse
CALL CancelChord("minor",root,channel)
CLOSE 1
END
REM End of the main section
REM -----------------------------------------------------------------
REM Subprograms and subroutines...
SUB PlayChord(type$,rootnote,channel) STATIC
   IF type$="major" THEN RESTORE MajorChord
   IF type$="minor" THEN RESTORE MinorChord
```

```
    READ count
    FOR I= 1 TO count
         READ interval
         PRINT#1,FNNoteOn$(rootnote+interval,channel)
    NEXT I
END SUB
REM  - - - - - - - - - - - - - - - - - - - - - - - - - - - - - - - - - - - - -
SUB CancelChord(type$,rootnote,channel) STATIC
   IF type$="major" THEN RESTORE MajorChord
   IF type$="minor" THEN RESTORE MinorChord
   READ count
   FOR I=1 TO count
         READ interval
         PRINT#1,FNNoteOff$(rootnote+interval,channel)
   NEXT I
END SUB
REM  - - - - - - - - - - - - - - - - - - - - - - - - - - - - - - - - - - - - -
CheckMouse: IF MOUSE(0)<>-1 THEN CheckMouse
RETURN
REM  - - - - - - - - - - - - - - - - - - - - - - - - - - - - - - - - - - - - -
```

It should be obvious from these discussions that once you know how to transmit one type of Midi message you can apply the same principles to any Midi message. Having to work with binary and hex numbers takes a bit of getting used to if you have not encountered them before. The solution if you have any difficulties in this area is to practice. Have a look in your synthesizer's Midi Implementation Chart or manual, see what types of messages the synthesizer can recognise, and then write a few of your own test programs. This type of experimenting will help you get to grips with these alien number forms in no time.

Collecting Midi Messages

Midi data arrives at the Amiga serial port as a series of byte (8-bit) values, and on the face of it a program simply has to read a byte as it arrives, use it, and then loop back to collect another byte, ad infinitum. In practice this approach turns out to be too simplistic because it disregards the fact that any given Midi byte is likely to be related to either preceding and/or succeeding bytes. Any Midi program which is going to do anything useful with the incoming data must be able to recognise and distinguish between all of the various classes of Midi information. This means recognising status and data bytes, being able to cope with real-time messages, and possibly running status as well.

To see the type of problems a Midi reader program faces, place yourself in the same position as you look at these six hex numbers...

91 ... 4D ... 40 ... 91 ... 4D ... 0 ...

Hex 91 is a note-on status byte. This tells us that two more data bytes—specifying the note and the velocity values—are going to arrive. With the above example the data bytes 4D and 40 complete the message. The 91 value of the fourth byte tells us that second note-on message is arriving, and the 4D and 0 values tell us that this message is actually going to turn a note off.

In analysing those six bytes we had to look for status bytes and had to identify the messages being dealt with. That was the only way we could tell how many data bytes would arrive. If you repeat the analysis with a stream of numbers that contains the odd real-time message thrown in, or a stream that is employing running status (the use of implied status bytes, that is), you'll appreciate that the analysis needs to be quite carefully controlled.

The top section of the Midi byte hierarchy is the status-byte/data-byte division. This is easy to deal with. Incoming bytes are either status bytes or data bytes, never both. Midi status bytes can be categorised in a similar, although slightly more involved fashion. Real-time messages, however, are tricky. Because they are time critical they can be inserted between the bytes of other Midi messages and this will be a complication that more sophisticated analysis programs need to deal with.

I'm not going to analyse the message structure arrangements used by Midi because that would take a book in itself. Instead I want to use the outline discussions already given, coupled with what we learnt about status bytes in the later chapters of this book, to create a simple Basic Midi status byte analyser program. It is not going to handle the large number of subclasses of controller messages which exist, but it will provide a useful starting point for further experiments and provide a piece of code that will be able to be used for a number of diagnostic purposes.

To collect serial data using HiSoft Basic on the Amiga a sequential file for input can be used like this...

```
OPEN "SER:" FOR INPUT AS #1 LEN=1
```

Data collection is then carried out by reading bytes one at a time using Basic's INPUT$() statement...

```
x$=INPUT$(1,1)
```

Normally it is more convenient to collect the value as a number rather than in string form and to do this it is convenient to opt for the combined use of the ASC() function...

```
x=ASC(INPUT$(1,1))
```

Using this collection statement in conjunction with a loop arrangement allows us to collect as much data as we want. To collect 100 Midi bytes we might use something along the lines of...

```
FOR i = 1 to 100
x=ASC(INPUT$(1,1))
...do something with the value in x...
NEXT i
```

Another simple scheme which could be used to continuously collect Midi data is...

```
forever=1
WHILE forever
x=ASC(INPUT$(1,1))
...do something with the value in x...
WEND
```

When collecting Midi bytes the first decision that will need to be made as each byte of information is received is whether it is a status byte or a data byte. This involves testing bit 7. I use the results of such tests to select between two subroutines like this...

```
IF (x AND &H80) THEN GOSUB STATUS.BYTE ELSE GOSUB DATA.BYTE
```

This line of code will distinguish between a status byte and a data byte but if a byte turns out to be a status byte then we'll need to know whether it is a channel status byte or a system message. The 1111 bit pattern in the upper part of the status byte signifies a system message and so this further test can be made...

```
IF (x<&HF0) THEN GOSUB CHANNEL.MESSAGE ELSE GOSUB SYSTEM.MESSAGE
```

What I am doing here is identifying the various Midi message classes, and on the basis of the results selecting particular subroutines which will carry out the processing associated with a particular message group.

The subroutine which receives channel message status bytes might isolate the channel and specific channel message class by using this type of bit-oriented code...

```
channel = (x AND &HF)+1
status = x AND &H70
...do something...
```

The easiest way to see how this message-subset/subroutine correspondence works is to put all the pieces together into a runnable program and this is exactly what the next listing provides. A 'forever' loop is used to collect the Midi bytes, status bytes are identified as either channel or system bytes and all channel byte values are sent to a routine which extracts their identification code and channel number and then uses that information to print details of the message received. Notice that by defining *CHANNEL.MESSAGE$()*, a message type string array whose used numerical array element positions correspond to the bit contents of the upper four bits of the message classes, I've made it easy to do the conversion from message class bit pattern to printed message class text name.

```
REM  - - - - - - - - - - - - - - - - - - - - - - - - - - - - - - - - - - - - - - - - - - - -
DIM CHANNEL.MESSAGE$(112)
CHANNEL.MESSAGE$(0)   = "Note Off"
CHANNEL.MESSAGE$(16)  = "Note On"
CHANNEL.MESSAGE$(32)  = "Poly Key Pressure"
CHANNEL.MESSAGE$(48)  = "Control Change"
CHANNEL.MESSAGE$(64)  = "Program Change"
CHANNEL.MESSAGE$(80)  = "Channel Pressure"
CHANNEL.MESSAGE$(96)  = "Pitch Bend"
CHANNEL.MESSAGE$(112) = "System Message"
REM  - - - - - - - - - - - - - - - - - - - - - - - - - - - - - - - - - - - - - - - - - - - -
OPEN "SER:" FOR INPUT AS #1 LEN=1
forever=1
WHILE forever
```

```
    x = ASC(INPUT$(1,1))
    IF (x AND &H80) THEN GOSUB STATUS.BYTE ELSE GOSUB DATA.BYTE
WEND
CLOSE 1
END
REM ---------------------------------------------------------------------
STATUS.BYTE:
    IF (x<&HF0) THEN GOSUB CHANNEL.MESSAGE ELSE GOSUB SYSTEM.MESSAGE
RETURN
REM ---------------------------------------------------------------------
CHANNEL.MESSAGE:
    channel = (x AND &HF)+1
    status = x AND &H70
    PRINT CHANNEL.MESSAGE$(status);" on channel ";channel
RETURN
REM ---------------------------------------------------------------------
SYSTEM.MESSAGE: RETURN
REM ---------------------------------------------------------------------
DATA.BYTE: RETURN
REM ---------------------------------------------------------------------
```

And There's More...

If you are happy with the logic behind the program just given it'll come as no surprise to you to find that we can easily adapt it to cater for the remaining status bytes, the system common and real-time status identifiers. The system message status bytes, that in the above listing are ignored, can be checked and on the basis of bit 3. We can execute one of two subroutines like this...

```
SYSTEM.MESSAGE:
    IF (x AND &H8) THEN GOSUB REAL.TIME.MESSAGE ELSE GOSUB COMMON.MESSAGE
```

By defining additional string arrays to hold the names of the various system and real-time messages, and relating the text entries to the appropriate bit patterns of the status bytes, it becomes easy to display the names of the status bytes as they are detected and so produce a usable diagnostic program. The next listing gives this expanded version and, once you understand how the nested subroutine status byte analysis scheme is used in conjunction with the bit patterns of the status bytes, you ought to be able to use a similar approach to create any number of Midi utility programs.

```
REM  - - - - - - - - - - - - - - - - - - - - - - - - - - - - - - - - - - - - - - -
DIM CHANNEL.MESSAGE$(112)
DIM COMMON.MESSAGE$(7)
DIM REAL.TIME.MESSAGE$(15)
CHANNEL.MESSAGE$(0) = "Note Off"
CHANNEL.MESSAGE$(16) = "Note On"
CHANNEL.MESSAGE$(32) = "Poly Key Pressure"
CHANNEL.MESSAGE$(48) = "Control Change"
CHANNEL.MESSAGE$(64) = "Program Change"
CHANNEL.MESSAGE$(80) = "Channel Pressure"
CHANNEL.MESSAGE$(96) = "Pitch Bend"
CHANNEL.MESSAGE$(112) = "System Message"
COMMON.MESSAGE$(0) = "System Exclusive"
```

```
COMMON.MESSAGE$(1) = "Midi Time Code"
COMMON.MESSAGE$(2) = "Song Position Pointer"
COMMON.MESSAGE$(3) = "Song Select"
COMMON.MESSAGE$(4) = "Undefined"
COMMON.MESSAGE$(5) = "Undefined"
COMMON.MESSAGE$(6) = "Tune Request"
COMMON.MESSAGE$(7) = "End of System Exclusive
REAL.TIME.MESSAGE$(0) = "Timing Clock"
REAL.TIME.MESSAGE$(1) = "Undefined"
REAL.TIME.MESSAGE$(2) = "Start"
REAL.TIME.MESSAGE$(3) = "Continue"
REAL.TIME.MESSAGE$(4) = "Stop"
REAL.TIME.MESSAGE$(5) = "Undefined"
REAL.TIME.MESSAGE$(6) = "Active Sensing"
REAL.TIME.MESSAGE$(7) = "System Reset"
REM ---------------------------------------------------------------
OPEN "SER:" FOR INPUT AS #1 LEN=1
forever=1
WHILE forever
   x = ASC(INPUT$(1,1))
   IF (x AND &H80) THEN GOSUB STATUS.BYTE ELSE GOSUB DATA.BYTE
WEND
CLOSE 1
END
REM ---------------------------------------------------------------
STATUS.BYTE:
   IF (x<&HF0) THEN GOSUB CHANNEL.MESSAGE ELSE GOSUB SYSTEM.MESSAGE
RETURN
REM ---------------------------------------------------------------
CHANNEL.MESSAGE:
   channel = (x AND &HF)+1
```

```
   status = x AND &H70
   PRINT CHANNEL.MESSAGE$(status);" on channel ";channel
RETURN
REM -----------------------------------------------------------------
SYSTEM.MESSAGE:
   IF (x AND &H8) THEN GOSUB REAL.TIME.MESSAGE ELSE GOSUB COMMON.MESSAGE
RETURN
REM -----------------------------------------------------------------
REAL.TIME.MESSAGE:
   PRINT REAL.TIME.MESSAGE$(x AND 7)
RETURN
REM -----------------------------------------------------------------
COMMON.MESSAGE:
   PRINT COMMON.MESSAGE$(x AND 7)
RETURN
REM -----------------------------------------------------------------
DATA.BYTE: RETURN
REM -----------------------------------------------------------------
```

Glossary

Accelerando

To gradually increase the tempo of a piece of music over a period of time.

Active

Multiple uses in the computer music and electronics world. Many computer programs which have options that can be turned on and off talk of options being active, turned on that is. With amplifiers and mixers there's a class of frequency filters known as active filters. They contain amplifying circuitry and the term active filters is used to distinguish them from alternative arrangements called passive filters, which do not require a power source and contain only resistors and capacitors.

Active Sensing

This is a special Midi message which enables pieces of equipment to check the Midi communications lines. It's a real-time message that consists of a single byte (decimal 254). Active sensing is a great idea although many products do not seem to implement it. Its purpose is to enable a piece of equipment to tell whether there has been a break in the Midi communications lines - faulty leads, units being accidentally unplugged etc.

The use of active sensing is optional, so if your units never receive an active sensing message they'll pretend it doesn't exist. Once a unit does receive active sensing information it will then expect to receive real Midi information, or at the very least an active sensing message, within 300 millseconds. As long as this data keeps coming everything is fine. If something goes wrong, say the data doesn't arrive, the equipment will turn off its sound producing circuitry and return to a 'just switched on' passive state.

AD Converter

An Analogue-to-Digital converter is a device which will convert an analogue signal—a continuously varying signal, that is—into a digital form consisting of a series of numbers. The numbers represent the amplitude—the strength or signal height—of the analogue signal at a particular point in time and here it's the speed and resolution of the A/D converter that determines the accuracy. It's these types of devices which allow sampling to be done and as the converter resolution increases the resulting digitized signal quality improves. 8, 12, and 16-bit A/D converters are the most common.

ADC

See A/D converter.

Additive Synthesis

A method of sound synthesis which uses simple sound waveforms as its starting point and combines them to make more complex sound arrangements.

ADSR

These initials stand for Attack, Decay, Sustain and Release. They represent four commonly found and adjustable sound generator characteristics. Synthesizer envelope generators usually have ADSR controls.

Aftertouch

Variation of the tonal quality of a note by pressure applied to a key during the time the key is held down. Nowadays most aftertouch sensitive keyboards can use the pressure variation to modulate signal frequency, amplitude, decay or any other waveform characteristic. The Midi standard defines two types of aftertouch messages—channel aftertouch and polyphonic aftertouch. Channel aftertouch provides an average value, an overall keyboard pressure value which is often called channel pressure. Polyphonic aftertouch provides pressure data for individual keys. This is potentially more expressive but is expensive to implement and can contribute to Midi clogging problems because of the large number of messages involved.

Algorithm

A step-by-step plan, a procedur, for solving a problem. Also used in the world of FM music-synthesis to imply a particular configuration, ie arrangement, of operators.

Algorithmic Composition

The process of generating music using a defined set of rules.

Aliasing

A distortion produced to some extent by all digital recording systems. It is caused by the harmonics of an audio signal clashing with the sampling frequency used in the digitizing process.

All Notes Off

A Midi message which tells the receiving unit to turn aff all notes currently sounding. It's a fail-safe message which is frequently sent as an insurance policy, especially just prior to messages—before sysyex or Mode messages for example—that might otherwise alter the reception characteristics of a unit whilst some notes are still sounding.

Alpha Dial

A round dial used on many Roland synthesizers for parameter selection. As the dial is rotated the digital display cycles through the available options. You move the dial until the required setting is seen in the display area.

Amplitude

The intensity width of a soundwave or signal.

Amplitude Modulation

A process whereby the amplitude of a signal is varied according to some cyclic, repetitive pattern. Tremolo effects are created by amplitude modulation.

Anti-aliasing Filter

Electronic filter designed to remove aliasing distortion.

Applications Software

General name for the non-system software programs that you run on a computer. Sequencers, notation programs, word processors and so on all constitute applications software.

Arpeggiator

A built-in electronic sequencer circuit, or sequencer program effect, that allows a melodic series of notes to be generated whilst just a single note is held down.

Assignable Controllers

This facility allows the controller numbers that govern certain effects (like modulation) to be chosen by the user. Usually only found on more expensive synthesizers.

Attack

The initial impact part of the sound. A percussion sound such as a cymbal voice will have a very prominent attack section which then fades rapidly away.

Attack Velocity

A measure of the rate at which a sound reaches its maximum initial impact.

Attenuation

Reducing the level of a signal.

Audio Sample

A digital copy of a real sound, based on a set of numbers representing the sound's amplitude measurements over a given period of time. This information is sufficient to allow the sound to be recreated electronically.

Autocorrect

A less common term for the quantize function found on sequencers.

Autolocate

The ability of a sequencer, drum machine etc, to move to a specific part of a song or sequence. Midi uses Song Position Pointer messages to specify the position.

Average Pressure

A Midi term representing a general measurement of how hard or how quickly keys have been pressed on a synth keyboard.

Balance

The ratio of the left and right portions of a stereo sound signal.

Bandwidth

A measurement of the range of frequencies that a particular type of electronic device can cope with.

Bank

Common term for a set of memory locations used to store voice characteristics and other settings in a synthesizer.

Bank Copying

Copying the sounds from one synthesizer memory bank to another.

Bank Select

Selecting a particular bank of synthesizer sounds.

Basic

A computer language for beginners.

Basic Channel

The fundamental channel of a Midi unit.

Baud

A unit of speed for serial communications.

Beats Per Minute

Common way of expressing the tempo of a piece of music.

Bend

To smoothly sharpen a note. A guitarist or other stringed instrument user can pull a string sideways. Synth players use an electronic pitchbend wheel or lever to produce a similar effect.

Bounce

To record a music track by copying an existing track whilst playing along with it. On two-track tape recorders this allowed multi-track recordings to be produced, although noise increased and therefore quality decreased each time this was done. Same type of thing can be done with Midi sequencers and, because there is no loss in quality, the process can be repeated as often as necessary.

BPM

Beats Per Minute

Buffer

Temporary storage area in a computer's memory.

C

A popular computer language used by many professional programmers.

Cannon Connector

A robust connecting terminal used in a lot of professional audio equipment. Also known as an XLR connector.

Channel

Midi uses a scheme that allows pieces of musical equipment to be given an identification number between 1 and 16. This provides 16 different 'communications lines' that musical equipment can use to talk to each other. These are known as Midi channels.

Channel Message

Any Midi message that contains a channel number.

Click Track

Simple guide track (straight fours on a hi-hat, for example) laid down on either a tape-recorder or sequencer to help a musician keep time.

Cut

Sequencer editing term meaning to remove a section from a sequence.

Cut-and-Paste

Sequencer editing term meaning to remove a section from a sequence and place it somewhere else.

CV

Control Voltage

Daisy Chaining

Linking Midi equipment so that the data travels through each unit in turn.

dB

Decibel. A unit used to represent sound level.

Default

A program value or electronic equipment setting that is available automatically at startup.

Doubling

Duplicating a melody line onto another track so as to enrich its sound.

Edit Buffer

Temporary storage area in computer memory where editing operations are carried out by a program.

Expander Module

The guts of a synthesizer built into a box without the keyboard.

File Format

The internal arrangement used for storing a particular type of data on a computer disk.

FM Synthesis

A method of sound synthesis used by many Yamaha synthesizers.

FX

Slang term for 'sound effects'.

Gain

The level of amplication applied to a signal.

Glide

Moving from one note to another smoothly.

Graphic Equalizer

A sophisticated 'mulltiple frequency band' tone control.

Humanize

To make a sequence or song sound less mechanical.

IMA

International Midi Asociation.

JMSC

Japan Midi Standards Committee.

Keyboard split

Where two or more areas of a synthesizer keyboard are configured so that the keys of the various zones generate messages on different Midi channels.

LCD

Liquid Crystal Display.

LED

Light Emitting Diode.

LFO

Low Frequency Oscillator.

Master keyboard

A synthesizer style Midi keyboard with no sound generating circuitry. Since these are especially designed to act as a master controller they include things like assignable controllers, Midi clock generators and so on.

Master volume

The control which adjusts the overall volume of a piece of equipment.

MMA

Midi Manufacturers Association.

Mother keyboard

Less common name for a master keyboard.

Portamento

Smooth glide between two or more notes.

ppqn

Pulses Per Quarter Note.

Running status

A mechanism used by Midi to eliminate the unnecessary transmission of duplicate status bytes.

Stripe

To record a sync track onto a reel of recording tape.

Sync

To keep in time with.

Tempo

The speed at which a piece of music is played.

Transpose

To change the key of a section or piece of music.

Transpose Protect

Sequencer facility which allows one or more tracks to be protected from general transpose edit operations. Used almost exclusively for drum tracks.

INDEX

INDEX

INDEX

presets synthesizer 14
program change 18, 54, 64, 111, 146
     tables 195
proximity hum 135

Q

quantization 32, 51, 60

R

radio 92
randomisation 77
real time messages 139
rechannelling 23, 65
remapping 54
Roland GS standard 111, 119
running status 239

S

sequence editing 53
sequencers 24, 49
serial ports 29
     tranmission 9
SMPTE/timecode 88
software 31
song position pointer 131, 141
song select 141
sound layering 65
sound modules (expanders) 15, 37,237
star networking 40
start message 49, 78, 139
status bytes 10, 144,161
stop messages 139
switch controllers 152
switcher boxes 45
Sync 24 (Roland) 97
synchronisation using Midi clocks 77
sysex events 188
     example 168

messages 165
system common messages 141
system reset messages 139

T

thru boxes 40
time shifting 65, 75
timecode 88
timing/clocks 33,51, 78, 131, 139
touch sensitive keyboards 15, 144
transmission parallel/serial 9
transpose protect 70, 240
transposition 63
tune request 141

V

velocity 144
voice messages 143
voice selection 18, 63

W

wireless Midi 92

NOTES

http://www.hisoft.co.uk

updates

special offers

latest news

easy ordering

tips & tricks

price lists

contacts

why aren't you there now?

ProMIDI Interface

Now your Amiga and your MIDI instruments can talk to each other

The ProMIDI Interface is a full, professional standard cartridge which is fully compatible with all MIDI keyboards, drum machines etc.

The attractive ProMIDI unit plugs into your Amiga's serial port, via high quality ribbon cable which minimises data loss, and incorporates MIDI-IN, MIDI-THRU and two MIDI-OUT ports, giving great flexibility.

There are distinct advantages to being able to position your MIDI Interface alongside your computer, rather than behind it, as it means that swapping cables from one MIDI device to another becomes a simple task.

The ProMIDI Interface is compatible with all MIDI software packages e.g. Bars and Pipes, Music X, Sequencer 1/Plus, Pro 24 etc.

The ProMIDI Interface is a proven product, already in use with many thousands of Amigas, from a company with over 10 years of experience in the computer music industry.

The package contains:

· ProMIDI Interface cartridge
· Disk containing many useful MIDI-related PD programs
· Complete manual with full set-up and program details

HiSoft, The Old School,
Greenfield, MK45 5DE.
Tel 01525 718181
Fax 01525 713716

All major credit cards accepted